BOOKS BY THOMAS GRAHAM BELDEN
AND MARVA ROBINS BELDEN

So Fell the Angels

The Lengthening Shadow

THE
LENGTHENING
SHADOW

Published simultaneously in Canada
by Little, Brown & Company (Canada) Limited

PRINTED IN THE UNITED STATES OF AMERICA

To Dorothy and Wood Gray

Denver, Colorado
August 22, 1949

DEAR TOM:

A thought that has occurred and reoccurred to me during my vacation is that some capable writer should do a biography of your life. This thought came to me because of my constant concern, publicly and privately, in the combating of the trend toward excessive paternalism in Government. As you know, I constantly preach individual initiative and acceptance of individual responsibility if we are in the long run to avert Statism. It seems to me that an account of your life would be a story of practicable achievement in the free enterprise system that would be far more effective in support of my argument than almost anything else could be.

You have been known as one of the liberal leaders of industry; your own personal record as well as that of your company under your leadership should bring home many lessons to the participants in the industrial strife that now plagues the nation.

There are undoubtedly many writers and scholars who would like to write a biography of you. It might even be done best as a "collaboration" effort by two or more writers.

In any event, it is my thought that maybe you will be sufficiently interested to talk it over with me when I am in New York.

Cordially,

IKE

Mr. Thos. J. Watson
International Business Machines
Madison Avenue at 57th Street
New York, New York

CONTENTS

CONTENTS

ILLUSTRATIONS

THE
LENGTHENING
SHADOW

1

BIRTH OF A SALESMAN

IBM is one of the most distinctive companies in America. The question is, How did it get that way? The answer, more than in most companies, lies in the personality of one man — its first president, Thomas J. Watson — and the story begins back in the 1890's.

It was late spring in the year 1892 when young Tom Watson drove away from Painted Post, New York. He was eighteen, and he was not sure where the road ahead would lead him. But he was satisfied. He had a job, and, as he said later, "I had the sense to know that was a pretty important thing for a young man to have."

He was going to like being a salesman. He had a good team of horses "and an organ wagon they called it, a great long wagon with a high seat in front and the top over it. On a stormy day there was a rubber curtain I could hang up in front and put the reins through a slot, fill my pipe, and I was in command, at least of that outfit." Everything about the life suited him, and although he was to be a salesman only eleven of his sixty-five years in business, he would never think of himself in any other role.

To be a wanderer was part of Watson's heritage. His father had been about his age when he took to the open road, and his family for generations had emigrated from the land of their birth, from Scotland to Ireland at the turn of the century, from Ireland to New York State about 1850, all but one of his uncles settling with his father in upper New York in the Susquehanna River valley, near the Pennsylvania border.

Change ran deep in the family blood. By the time the boy was of age he had lived in at least five houses in the area, and even his name had been altered. Born Thomas John Wasson on February 17, 1874, he was now Thomas J. Watson. The family had been Watsons in Scotland and Watsons in Ireland; but, when a relative settled in Brooklyn and married a Catholic, the other members of the family, being Presbyterian and Irish in their attitude toward religion (while militantly refusing to consider themselves Irish in anything else), changed their name to Wasson to disassociate themselves from Rome. Whatever his own feelings may have been, Watson's father had gone along with the others for about thirty years; but the name WATSON was tattooed on his arm, and by the time his boy began his career, the old lumberman had asserted his independence and changed his family's name back to the original spelling. Watson the boy now was, and different somehow from the others.

He had made a few false starts in finding himself. As a

youth he had worked on the family farm training horses, harvesting, topping trees, driving the team that pulled the stoneboat. But the land was poor, so poor, one of his neighbors said, "that you couldn't even raise a disturbance on it," and farming did not appeal to him. His father, a brusque, practical man with little education himself, was ambitious for his only son and wanted him to study law, but Watson rebelled against the suggestion.

At that time, as he was to observe later, "I was absolutely sure that I was a smarter man than my father. I was positive of that. I felt that I could prove it, if I were called upon to prove it."

"What are you going to do now? What have you got in mind?" his father asked.

Watson said, "I've decided to teach school." He meant to get a certificate, teach for three years, then go to Albany Teacher's College. But after a day of being a substitute teacher, he concluded, "That settles my teaching career. I can't go into a schoolroom with a bunch of children at nine o'clock in the morning and stay till four."

When he told his father that he had changed his mind and decided to go into business, his father did not, as young Watson feared, send him out to work on the farm. Now the young man was all impatience with education. He did not want to go to Cornell or anywhere to business school; he wanted to go to work immediately. But on this point his father won out, and Watson spent a year studying business and accounting at a small local business college, the Miller School of Commerce, about twenty miles to the east, in Elmira. When he graduated in May, 1892, he was offered a job as bookkeeper at six dollars a week by Clarence Risley, who ran a meat market in Painted Post, where Watson's family now had a house on High Street. The salary was good, and Watson took the job. But he soon found, he said, "that I couldn't sit on a high stool and keep books all my life."

After he had been posting accounts for a few weeks, Watson met a young newcomer to town at a Sunday-school picnic. His name was George Cornwell, and he had come to Painted Post to sell pianos, organs, and sewing machines for the Bronsons, an enterprising local family. It was a good business, Cornwell told Watson, and he needed an assistant. That very night Watson went off to see about getting the job. Bronson, his Sunday-school superintendent, said fine, he would take him on at ten dollars a week if he could provide his own horses. To Watson the salary seemed more than generous. Having been born under the cloud of the Panic of 1873, he could remember large families getting along on half the amount.

He took the job, and he and Cornwell started out. They had high-spirited horses and dandy rigs – Watson's bright yellow organ wagon, a "democrat wagon," it was called, and another smaller wagon for their sewing machines. They would appear at all the local country fairs, trotting up in style and setting up shop in their wagons. Or they might go off to a near-by village, set up store for a few weeks, then, when they had sold all the pianos and organs they could, move on. They slept at farms along the way or in one of the villages, where always they were cousins or friends. Often they would bring their pianos in with them and, after an evening of playing chords with the family gathered round, would drive off with a sale. One of Watson's sisters played the piano for the Sunday school, but he was tone deaf and unmusical and had to depend on Cornwell or a friend to compare a Chickering and Steinway piano or play the Estey organs.

Watson's new life was not always easy. The road was long, his hours were long, and so were his chances. In spring came the inevitable floods, and the heavy, clumsy wagons would get mired down in mud. In winter the roads were knotted with ice, and the boys sometimes took to the local lakes to save time, rides that were daring and exhilarating, but dangerous, dark, and cold. A year after Watson started out in business, there was a serious recession, which took, as one of his friends said, all they had except their adolescence and their tight hatbands.

But it was a good life, and Watson thrived. Railroads and canals linked Steuben County to East and West, but most of the land was rural and beautiful. To the north were the Finger Lakes, a splayed hand reaching toward Pennsylvania, and the land was furrowed with rivers running through rough-backed hills, still wooded and free. It was a boy's paradise, but it was Watson the man who began to love it, not so much the land itself, but the open road through it.

Being on the move gave him something he had never had before, a sense of belonging that other boys in the neighborhood had found roaming the hills together. Watson was never strong and athletic like his father, a brawny, fierce-looking Irishman with black beard and dark, angry eyes. The older man had always been able to take care of himself in any lumber-camp brawl, but his son, afflicted from childhood with asthma, did not even know how to swim, nor did he take to hunting and fishing like his friends. He was a lively, assertive boy, expressing his energy in a quick temper and pranks, but there was always a suggestion of restraint in him, and even at parties he sometimes had a speculative look, strained and dissatisfied, as if he had drawn apart and was measuring himself. When he graduated from high school he was thin, and there was a look of uncertainty in his eyes. But after a few months on the road his big thin frame began to fill out, and he became, perhaps to his own surprise, a handsome fellow, a Gibson hero, over six feet tall — straight and strong and confident.

Watson used to say that he held the horses while Cornwell made the sales in those early days. Actually they took turns with their prospects, but his partner's approach made Cornwell impatient. Watson enjoyed meeting people too much to stick to business, and he would just as soon discuss crops all day with a farmer as get down to the matter at hand. He learned a lot about people in those days, and he learned something about business, too, because, as he said, "Mr. Bronson never paid anyone for loafing."

An organ cost him about a third what it cost the farmer, but the trick was to finish up each week with enough cash to pay Bronson for his wares. Watson sometimes had trouble because to sell, he had to barter, and along with some cash he might get a cow for a sewing machine, or butter and oats or a colt for a piano. Sometimes, when a calf was spindly or the butter substandard, his mother had to help him out, feeding his stock and rechurning the butter before he could sell his acquisitions for cash. Along with the rest of his family he took pride in his knowledge of horses and liked to think he knew how to make a good trade on the road, but even there he was sometimes fooled and had to ride out a wild team.

Watson grew shrewd, seeing that good business was a bargain that benefited both parties, the Golden Rule of business he never forgot. It was a lesson he had to learn to survive in the days when he needed the good exchange as much as the farmer. And it was a lesson that would stand him in good stead when business was lifted from the community of friends, relatives, and neighbors to a national scale; for, in a sense, the mass market was to create a neighborhood stretching from Long Island Sound to San Francisco Bay. The corporation might replace the man and his buggy, but in the days of big business a good name would still be a good name, and virtues once legislated by proximity would still hold, and integrity remain the best drummer.

Cornwell soon left for a better job, leaving Bronson a store filled with wares. "So he called me in and turned it over to me," Watson recalled as an old man, "and that was the most responsible job I've ever had from that day to this. And I felt more important in it than any position I've ever held, because I was the general manager, sales manager, accountant, deliveryman — I was the whole organization."

He was good, too, and the town druggist, who had a

store next to Bronson's, used to say, "Tom, you always come back empty. Where do you store all the stuff?" But Bronson never gave him a raise or a compliment for two years.

One day another organ salesman said to Watson, "You're doing well. What's your salary?"

"Twelve dollars a week," said Watson, pleased with his advance.

"What?" exclaimed the salesman indignantly. "That's awful!"

No, Watson said, that was a good rate, one of the best in town. His friend pointed out to him that working on commission he would be earning about six times that amount.

The next morning Watson took his time getting to work and, when he arrived, announced that he was quitting. Bronson, taken aback, offered him a raise and finally a chance to buy the business if he would sign a note. Watson took the proposition to his father, but he said no.

The young man did not think very much of his father's business ability. "I guess my father was never meant to be a rich man," he remarked dryly afterward. He had worked for years in the lumber industry in that part of the country, then center of one of the largest timbering operations in the country, but compared to other men in the community like Bronson he had not made much money. Part of his trouble was bad luck. When he got married in his late thirties, he settled down for a few years on a small farm near East Campbell, New York, to raise tobacco and grain, but before he had made any success of the project, his farmhouse burned down. Eventually he was forced to combine farming with a small lumbering business, buying up the second-growth timber, mostly hemlock, that was left in the area and sawing it up with his portable steam saw. In the year of the great Johnstown flood, local rivers overflowed and inundated his lumberyards, leaving him almost nothing to salvage when they receded.

By 1894, fire flood, and a national recession had left Watson's father little but advice to give his son, but what he had was good; and whatever Watson's opinion of his father's judgment at the time, he would always thank him for it afterward. Leave Painted Post, his father said. He might make a living there, but it was no place to spend a lifetime. And so Watson turned down Bronson's offer and, instead of buying the business, helped Bronson sell it. Then he said good-by to his relatives and friends and once again took to the road, this time heading west toward Buffalo.

Watson would never regret leaving home, but he would never renounce it, and years later he would recall nostalgically the evocative Indian names of the place — Tioga, Cohocton, Chemung, Canisteo, reminiscent of the days when the area was occupied by the Senecas. He would always proudly claim the village of Painted Post as his birthplace, even though it was not. "As a matter of fact, I was born in a neighboring village, [East] Campbell," he would admit, "but people regard me with greater interest because Painted Post conjures up images of redskins, arrows, and scalping." The name of the village supposedly originated with a monument raised by the Indians to one of their heroes in their battle with the moving frontier, but Watson preferred the less likely but more lively story that the original painted post had been a brag post, erected by the Indians as a place to celebrate past victories and those to come. There was some truth in his version, for in his time the old column had been replaced by a sheet-iron Indian on which the young men of the town wrote their names, thereby appropriating the town monument to themselves and what they meant to be. Watson, more than the others, had a tendency to put his name on things in a large bold hand, on the monument many times and, more conspicuously than anyone else, on the stairway leading up to the town's public hall.

Painted Post was far from being the lively place its name suggested, as Watson knew, but somehow that quiet, shabby village bequeathed him a complicated heritage, stirred up fires in a boy's heart. His fellow villagers would be surprised at the man the boy grew up to be.

But Painted Post, population 600, with its lumber and flour mills and handful of stores, did not prepare Watson for the raw, thriving port of Buffalo, nor did his selling experience in his own neighborhood equip him to go into the economic wilderness of the 1890's. For six weeks he wandered around trying to find a job, and when he finally got one with the Wheeler and Wilcox Company selling sewing machines, he had almost nothing left in his pocket. His feeling of relief was short-lived; for, not long after he began traveling about the countryside with his sewing machines, the company decided it could do without his services, and he was once again without a job.

Watson learned one valuable lesson from the experience.

The peddlers he came across in the little towns outside of Buffalo were a different lot from Cornwell and Bronson. Cast free from family ties, these men were rootless, hard-eyed wanderers, always on the lookout for the unfamiliar road. They claimed no cousins along the way. Travel offered anonymity along with loneliness; and with no ac-counting to do except to the head office, they elected to do most of their business where they took their pleasure — in saloons. Watson learned the price they paid, and the in-struction burned into his mind. In subsequent years he was to see many careers ruined by drinking, but after a few weeks on the road for Wheeler and Wilcox, it was never to be a threat to him personally. And he was to do more than any other businessman in America to divorce drink-ing from business. When accused of being too evangelical in the matter, he defended himself vigorously, saying that liquor had no part in a businessman's life, especially that of an executive. When an executive drinks, he said, "it is seri-ous because he is establishing that as part of his policy," and he added that he refused to waste his time reforming grown men, but he would go a long way to reform a young one.

In his brief career with Wheeler and Wilcox, Watson was impressed with one of his fellow salesmen, an older and, in Watson's eyes, a worldly fellow named C. B. Barron. He left the company at about the same time Wat-son did, and it was probably he who suggested that they get into a new line, the financial business. The Buffalo Building and Loan Association was opening branches in near-by villages, and salesmen were needed to sell stock to finance the expansion. Watson knew nothing of this kind

of operation, but Barron said that he had had some experience in such matters, and the two of them started out to
see what could be done.

Their first stop was Silver Creek, and the reception was
disappointing. Barron went off to their hotel in disgust,
but Watson walked over to the local saloon to try out his
sales talk on the men around the bar. They laughed at him.
When the bartender came over to console him, Watson's
spirits picked up, and he sold the man enough stock to
earn two dollars' commission. Afterward he went into a
tailor shop nearby and made a commission of five dollars.
Business really started to roll then, and Watson, between
Wednesday and Sunday, made one hundred and sixty-
nine dollars in commissions. It was, Watson said in awe
later, "more money than I ever thought any man could
make. . . ."

Now Watson had a chance to observe Barron operating.
He was quite a fellow, this Barron, wise in the ways of the
territory, a veteran traveling man, combination city slicker,
confidence man, genial cheat. To Barron the life of a salesman was a far cry from riding through the countryside
talking to friends and relatives. He preferred revisiting
towns infrequently, if at all, and the fewer people he knew,
the fewer things he had to prove. No, being a salesman to
him was a game, and a slick one at that. Travel fast and travel
light. The territory is wide open, and the head office sees
only the returns — not always those.

As for salesmanship, it was nothing but showmanship to
Barron. Sell yourself, and you sell your product was his approach, and more important than his knowledge of the rail-

pening with the company. Watson was more
impressed than Range, and besides, he could not
r job that suited him. Twice he went back, and
October, 1895, he talked himself into a job,
f a regular salesman, but one that would give
ce to prove himself.

was leaving town to attend a convention, and
time to do was to hand the boy a company
ying, "You study that and I'll put you on a
Monday." Watson found himself with the
er, the first canned sales approach in America.
re, experience had taught the company presi-
H. Patterson, disrespect for the haphazard man-
drummer, relying for his income on charm,
ullibility; and he had set about remedying affairs
acteristically methodical fashion. He looked up
ny's best money-earner, had his sales talk re-
rd for word, and in 1887 presented it to his
les force. Thereafter it was to be the only one
salesmen, he decreed. The primer was to be
rote, and the customer was to hear nothing else.
force, men of native arrogance who considered
alities their capital, were shocked at the heresy,
on's attitude was, "There never was a man free
pleased. You've got to do as others want you, or
ess." And so his men, perspiring uncomfortably,
ine, and they began making money, setting a
record in the depression of 1893 when Watson
hard time getting a piano off his democrat
the time Watson arrived in the NCR, the

roads and hotels from Penn Yan to Johnstown was his
appreciation of a gesture, his knowledge of the signs of afflu-
ence. Appearance is reality, he proclaimed. It doesn't matter
what you have in your pocket, only what you have in your
hand.

Forced to ride into town unheralded, without the au-
thenticity created by advertising, Barron traveled his territory with the glory of a comet. He would go off to
the best hotel, sign the register with a flourish, buy himself an expensive cigar (which he always took care to
smoke in public), and stroll into dinner. With his last dollar he would tip a bellboy to page him there when the
room was crowded, thereby establishing himself as a man
of urgent business responsibilities. As he leaned back after
dinner with a studied air of preoccupation, he would probably reflect that the next day, if everything went well, he
would be able to afford another cigar.

Yes, Barron knew how to make the most of things,
and Watson learned a great deal from him without becoming like him. And in time Watson was to do as much
as anybody in American business to make the Barrons obsolete.

But for a while Watson was fooled. He liked the brassy
flair of the man. And he envied him his tailor. Those were
the days, as Watson said, when the "salesmen of promise wore silk hats, cutaway coats, steel gray trousers,
carried canes, and rambled around the countryside. . . .
I was too young to dress that way," he added, but the
truth of the matter was that as soon as he made a little
money on the road he, too, would dress like a gentleman

with high button shoes, tall silk hat, and striped pants. He had always liked fancy clothes. In his school days his suit may have been plain and his collar ill-fitting, but even then his tie was bold, and he spent his spare money on silk store shirts. During his first two years in business he owned only one suit, but he took care that no one should notice, waiting patiently in the back of a tailor's shop while it was pressed and cleaned. As Watson said, "Clothes don't make the man, but they go a long way toward making a businessman." Barron it was who brought to full flowering this Cinderella principle of business.

Behind the splendid pose that Watson admired, Barron was a ne'er-do-well, likable but dishonest, and Watson's promising career in the world of finance came to an abrupt end when Barron disappeared with all the funds. The disaster came hard to the young man, for he had just failed in another venture. When the building and loan business was booming and he was making more money than he needed to live on, he had decided to go into business for himself. "At the time I had been reading a fascinating story about Thomas B. Hunter of Philadelphia, who was the first to start a chain of food stores," Watson said. "He started with three hundred and fifty dollars and had built up a tremendous number of stores. That appealed to me. . . ."

Borrowing money from his father, Watson established a butcher shop in a residential section of Buffalo. "I had a very sound plan," he explained. "I was going to keep right on working for this finance company and make money and start more stores until I had perhaps more than

Thomas B. Hunter. F
we got around to sta
first one."

In later years there
about his experience v
the building and loan
balloon ascensions tha
add, "and that was a
time it was not easy
had started out to se
had nothing to show
broke, and once du
been reduced to slee
ment of a store.

"They say money
he was an old man. "
big something when
world and haven't

After Barron, the
cation was a big,
his grocery busines
one being a second
brash, implacable e
road; but even that
to go down to the
Register Company
to his successor. W
would apply for a
was Range. He lo

was no o
favorably
get anothe
finally, in
not that c
him a char

Range
all he had
booklet, s
week from
NCR Prin
Years befc
dent, John
ners of th
luck, and g
in his char
the compa
corded wo
skeptical s
for NCR
learned by

The sales
their person
but Patters
to do as he
do no busin
came into
sensational
had had a
wagon. By

primer was company liturgy, and being young and ambitious, he learned the standard approach so well that he never forgot it as long as he lived.

It soon proved to be inadequate. Turned loose in his assigned territory, Watson roamed around for ten days without making a sale. Finally, one morning as he was leaving the office, Range stopped him and said, "Sit down, young man, and tell me what you have been doing."

"He took me by surprise," Watson recalled later, "and for a moment I did not know what to say. Then I told him I had been working, and I said, 'I haven't got any orders, but I have some good business in sight.'

"He said, 'In sight? How far away is it? Can I see it? Don't you ever waste my time talking about business that's in sight. I am not interested until you can show it to me in the form of a signed order.'"

When Watson said he was having trouble finding customers, Range barked, "Well, that is what I hired you for — to find them. You just haven't gone far enough. Keep going. If at five o'clock you have not found anyone, go on until six o'clock or until the stores close at nine if necessary. There is somebody in your territory who will buy a cash register if you are willing to go far enough to find him. It does not require a genius to find people who need these machines. Walking and talking are all that is necessary. Most of us can talk, but some of us are a little shy on walking. Keep going long enough, and you will find enough people who will say 'yes' to make you a success in this business."

Just as Watson had concluded that as soon as Range

stopped burning him up, he would quit, suddenly Range's whole bearing changed, and with his easy Irish smile he said, "Now, young man, I know what you're up against. I have been all through it. I know just what's happened to you. . . . Nearly everybody you have called on has said, 'I don't want a cash register.' Now, we all know that, because, if they decided they wanted a cash register, they would come down to the office and buy it. They wouldn't need any salesman. Now, let's take a different tack. . . . We'll put one on the rig and go out together and call on your best prospects. If we fall down, we'll fall down together, and then I cannot find any fault with you."

In over sixty years in business, nothing that happened to Watson had a greater impact on him than that experience with Range. Range knew that the time to tell a man harsh truths is when he is down. But a man who is down is not a salesman, and Range knew how to pick him up again. From him Watson learned his technique of ripping a man apart and sewing him up again, as he was to call it. And he learned how to sell.

Range was an old-fashioned salesman who had taken to the road with no primer under his arm; and he taught Watson to temper orthodoxy with his own good sense, showing him that, along with system, a salesman needed quick wits, good timing, and judgment. He made sales by leaning over the counter talking politics or swapping stories over crackers and coffee after hours, and when prospects told him no, they did not want a cash register, Range replied cheerfully, "I know you don't. What I've come for is to find out why you don't want one." Four times he went out with Watson, helping him load a big nickel-plated machine on his rig, and four times he closed an order.

By then Watson was ready to go out on his own, and three months later, in January, 1896, he became a full-fledged salesman. With his new position came certain privileges, some unique to the National Cash Register Company, or the Cash, as it was called. The guaranteed territory was one. The cash register had been a private enthusiasm when Patterson took over the company in 1883. In the previous five years only about one hundred machines had been sold, and it was said that Patterson had to offer a guaranteed territory to men to induce them to work for him at all. The policy did not catch fire in American industry, most companies preferring to put several men in an area to provide the spur of intracompany rivalry. Patterson, on the other hand, went so far to protect his salesmen's sovereignty that, if the factory sold a machine in Watson's territory, Watson got the commission.

And the commissions were good. Watson remembered the days in Painted Post when a friend told him he had just made thirty dollars selling a cash register, almost as much money as Watson was then making in a month. Someone accused the fellow of being the biggest liar in the Cohocton Valley, but he went right on making money, and Watson never forgot the incident. And if he still wanted to be in business for himself, and he did, selling on commission was just that. "It's You, Incorporated," as he said, with someone else providing the capital, and, in the case of the National Cash Register Company, much more besides.

Watson started on the west side of Buffalo, but before long he was working outside the city; and after nearly four years with Range he knew all the villages as far as the Ohio line and deep into Pennsylvania. When he was an old man, he still delighted in naming them off: Erie and Corry, Warren, Meadville and Olean, Titusville and Oil City. Then there were Salamanca, Cattaraugus, Mayville at the head of Lake Chautauqua, Westfield, Brockton, Silver Creek.

And if he instinctively loved the music of their names, he soon learned to respect their economic value as well. There had been a time when Range looked over letters from the head office inquiring about the small towns in his territory, nodded with good-natured superiority, and turned back to the city streets of Buffalo. Only when he was threatened with losing some of his jurisdiction did he sigh philosophically and say, "Tom, maybe you ought to hitch up a horse and buggy and take a trip through that territory." Watson and a shoe salesman loaded up a buggy together and started out. "We were gone twenty-one days, and in that time I sold twenty-one cash registers," Watson said later. "Up to that time no one had ever averaged one sale a day for every day in a seven-day week."

By the beginning of 1897 Watson was doing well, drawing as much as one hundred dollars a week against his commissions (advances being another unusual company policy), once drawing an all-time high of $1,225. "I didn't work myself to death, either, I will admit that," he said. "But when I worked, I worked."

Then, that spring, another business recession hit the

country, and his sales dropped more than a third, finally dwindling away to nothing in August. By the first of November he had still not made a sale. It was at times like these that Range would take over. Seeing Watson had had a bad week, he would say to him in an offhand way, "You know, I'm getting a little fed up with things in Buffalo. Why don't you invite me to come down and spend a week with you in your territory?" Watson always invited him down, and together they made some of the best records Watson ever had.

Business picked up the next year, and by October, 1898, his third anniversary with the company, Watson's record for the first time was the best in his office. In the following months he stayed at the top, sometimes tying with Range, more often beating him. Watson was ready for bigger things.

On the first of August, 1899, he became sales agent for the Rochester office. "I was twenty-five at that time," he said, "and the reason I was given that territory was that nobody else would take it." He found out why as soon as he arrived in town. As he was tying his horse to the hitching post in front of his new office, the saloonkeeper next door came out to greet him and told him the whole discouraging story — drunken agents, poor service, dissatisfied customers. Watson might have left in low spirits if he had not managed to sell the man an expensive two-drawer machine. On his way to call on one of his local complaining customers he sold another. "That sort of braced me up a little," he said.

And so he began. The going was not easy. A sales agent

got 35 per cent commission compared to the salesman's 15 per cent, but out of that amount he had to pay all of the operating expenses of his office. Watson was in Rochester two years before he could afford to draw more than twenty-five dollars a week for himself. "I had to count my pennies," he said, especially as he found himself taking over the support of his family.

For some years his father had not been well enough to run a sawmill; and when Watson settled in Buffalo, his family had left Painted Post and followed him there, going back to their farm in Steuben County only during the summers. His father continued to do some estimates of timberland and occasionally some horse trading, and his four sisters, strong-willed, competent women, taught school; but it was now Watson who held the family together. It never occurred to him that it should be otherwise.

When he got his promotion, the family came along and moved with him into a rented house in Arundel Park near Rochester. His sister Jennie worked as his assistant. Occasionally he had a salesman working for him, too; but in the early months none of them lasted very long, and Jennie and Tom made things go. Once, when she sold two cash registers, he bought her a diamond ring in celebration.

It was a tribal, gregarious family. When Watson's oldest sister, Effie, married an NCR salesman, he moved in with the rest. Watson sometimes complained good-naturedly that someday he wanted a house with a bathroom of his own, but basically he liked the arrangement. He had never known privacy, and would never want it. In later years, when people commented on his crowded, public life, he would always reply in a puzzled tone, "But I don't ever want to be alone."

Although he made little money for himself, Watson far surpassed the expectations of his company during his first year in Rochester. By the company's method of rating agencies, comparing performance with quota, Watson's office stood near rock bottom when he began, but in three months he was sixth, with over one hundred and fifty offices below him, and he stayed near the top the rest of the year. But he did not do so well his second year, when he dropped below his quota, slipping into the anonymous middle ranks of the company or, worse, appearing at times near the bottom of the roster. The reason was that for the first time in his life he was coming up against strong competition.

When John H. Patterson went into the cash register business, he acquired a monopoly, mainly because no one was interested in buying his strange machine, much less in manufacturing it. But by 1900, the NCR estimated there was a cash register for every four hundred people in the country, and by 1902 the company was producing a machine every fifteen minutes of the work week. Patterson's success encouraged others, and before long the company was fighting a lively battle with its competition on all fronts — in the courts, the press, and the stores of customers. Few competitors survived Patterson's displeasure for long, but one — the Hallwood Company — flourished, at least in a few cities. One was Rochester; and, once Watson had his own house in order, Hallwood became his major problem. Hallwood men began observing a tall, distinguished-looking fellow standing outside their office on Main Street. It was young Thomas Watson, wearing his few years well with a mustache and dignified bearing, and he would stand and stare and ruminate and then go off.

The market place was a jungle in those days, and salesmen had to dress like gentlemen, but know how to survive. There were all sorts of sharp and subtle ways of meeting competition, and there was the straightforward strong-arm method. In the cash register business, for instance, it was useful to have a working knowledge of the competitor's machine so that, under certain circumstances, it could be kept from working. Doubts about these practices were abroad in the NCR, and by Watson's day an occasional salesman was heard to proclaim that the clash of arms had to come to an end. Not everyone, particularly everyone of importance, agreed, but Watson did, and he would have something to do with settling the debate in later years. Style was as important to him as it had been to Barron, but with Watson style ran deep. In Rochester he was known as a rough customer, but a square shooter in the trade.

There were incidents he regretted. One time, hearing from his competitor that he had a prospect to see the next day, Watson got up at dawn, drove about twenty miles to the store, and was sitting on the porch with his cash register when the proprietor arrived. Watson got the order, and as he was leaving, he met the other salesman coming to make his call.

"You're up pretty early, Tom," the man said.

"Yes," Watson replied, "I had a job to do."

Feeling very good, he went over to the local hotel to have breakfast, but what at first had looked like a triumph troubled him in later years. The competitor was, after all, a friend, too. Watson boasted about the incident, telling the story over and over again, but eventually he was to say, "I will regret that until the day I die." Finally he stopped telling the story altogether.

For the most part he was satisfied with his record in Rochester. "I gathered some fellows around me, and when I left that territory, it was one of the best organized and cleanest territories that had ever been turned over to another man," Watson said. The head of the Hallwood office finally admitted defeat, saying he might as well try to make money playing poker.

For all the pressure of business, there were many times in those early days when Tom Watson took off his stovepipe hat, put aside his dignity, and had a good time. One of his best friends in town was Charles F. Ames, who had just begun working for the Eastman Kodak Company when Watson arrived. Ames was a likable fellow, and he and Watson soon struck a bargain: Watson with his favorite horse Dexter and fancy rig was to provide transportation on land, and Ames with his sloop *The Teaser* was to provide it on water. They made a lot of friends with the combination.

Watson was happy then in a way he could never be in the future, with responsibility and position weighing heavily upon him. As a businessman he made his philosophy out of looking to the future, and he had a certain pragmatic contempt for what was finished and done, but he cherished his own past as a salesman with deep feeling, refusing to relinquish his ties with it long after they had ceased to have meaning for others. He liked the chancy trade, the men he worked with, the customers, and long hours on the road. Those years burned in his mind, and when he was eighty, he would still be able to recall the sales he had made — the name of the shopkeeper, where his store was, in Buffalo or Rochester or Meadville, even the time of day he wrote up the order. "I like to tell this story. I like to hear it myself," he would say as he settled back to revive those golden times, and even after he became an international leader in business he was never too busy to sit down and, with surprising warmth and feeling, reminisce with an old NCR salesman he had not seen in twenty years.

He might have been content with the life forever if something had not occurred to concentrate his restless energies, to discipline and control them — a vision of what he might become.

It came in an unexpected way. He and a friend saved their money until they could afford a vacation at a resort in the Adirondacks, but their stay there was disappointing, and Watson left, determined never again to travel until he could afford the best. While there, he met a Chicago businessman who invited him to stop off in that city sometime and visit him. Watson did shortly afterward and found that the man lived in a magnificent house. When he looked about him and expressed his admiration, his host smiled and said he had started life on a farm. The thought leaped to Watson's mind that he, too, might someday have a home like that. He would, he decided, if he had a chance.

That chance came in October, 1903, when he was summoned to the head office in Dayton, Ohio. His father was dying, and he did not want to leave him; but reassured by the family doctor, he left, traveling all night and arriving at the NCR headquarters the next morning.

Mr. Patterson wanted to see him, he was informed, and he was ushered into the inner office for the first time, for the first time meeting Patterson face to face. Watson, nervous and confused, had little time to glance around the room, small, neat, Spartan in its furnishings. Nor did he have time to study the short, erect man with mild manners and blazing eyes who was John H. Patterson.

The proposition was immediately put to him. The company was threatened by competition from secondhand dealers trading with NCR machines. In the early days secondhand cash registers had been no problem; but the success of the NCR in producing long-lasting machines had eventually produced the disturbing situation of competitors making a lively profit selling NCR products. Company officials had decided to take a drastic step – to organize and finance a separate company with the intention of taking control of all the secondhand business in cash registers in the country. The operation was to be big, expensive — and entirely secret. No one was to know of its connection with the National Cash Register Company.

The moral right of the NCR to take that action, or any other for that matter, against other companies selling cash registers was without question in Patterson's mind. He was the pioneer in the field, he had created the demand for cash registers with his own ingenuity and hard work, and the field was his, he felt. "The best way to kill a dog is to cut off his head," Patterson said. He meant to put those other men out of business.

Watson was to run the whole affair, he was informed crisply.

He had been chosen for this delicate mission from more than four hundred salesmen of the company, not by Patterson, but by the new general manager, young Hugh Chalmers. Chalmers had known Watson for some years, had once even shared a commission with him; but Watson could not account for his dazzling ascent from the obscurity of his small agency by friendships in the head office. He knew Chalmers only slightly, and if he had ever seen the other major company officials before, he had had but a glimpse of them over the heads of the crowd at a company convention he attended in Dayton the year after he took over the Rochester office. His obscurity was, in fact, one of the recommendations that had brought him to Dayton a second time, for to keep its secret the NCR needed someone relatively unknown, someone with experience like Watson's with Hallwood, but someone who could draw apart from the NCR without arousing suspicion.

Watson left for Rochester that night; and when he arrived home the next morning, his mother met him at the door to tell him that his father was failing. Watson had time to tell him what had happened in Dayton, about the promotion, the big responsibilities and opportunity that lay before him.

His father said, "Well, I'm very pleased about that because what you have been doing hundreds of men can do, but now you're doing something different — something new — it's a great opportunity."

Watson said yes, it was a responsible job, that he would have a great deal of money — he said a million dollars — to spend according to his judgment, without the need to account for it in detail.

"This is a very fine thing for you," his father replied. "I know you will handle it right. I am going to give you some advice. Before you spend a dollar of your company's money, consider it as your own dollar. Do not ever spend any of your company's money when you would not spend your own money."

That evening his father died. It comforted Watson to realize that his father had lived long enough to know that he would be a success in business, that he was already on the way. Their relationship had not always been easy. The senior Watson was stern and domineering, and both were fiery, quick-tempered men, strong in their opinions, and proud. But the end was right, and Watson went to his father's funeral in silk top hat and tails because, he said, his father would have wanted him dressed that way.

The young man had come to a crossroads. At twenty-nine he buried his father, and for the first time he really left home. He had been well tutored — Painted Post teaching him the feel of the road and the mode of the bargain, Barron showing him a little of the art of appearance (and something about disappearance), the NCR the method, and Range the art of being a salesman. Now Watson was ready to begin his career on a national scale.

2

THE CASH

BECAUSE OF bad times the NCR had to reduce operations drastically from 1903 to 1904; but even during that first hard year in the secondhand business Watson flourished. "My whole success in the NCR was not due to my ability as a salesman," he observed later, adding, "and I had the record of being a pretty good salesman." He was, he now discovered, a better executive.

It was rough business. Watson established stores next to successful competitors, copied their successes, discarded their failures, hired their salesmen, undersold them, eventually put them out of business. His experiences during those years Watson always regretted and rarely mentioned afterward, but in many ways his success then was a unique and commendable triumph, his personal triumph over the accepted practices of his time. He always won, to be sure, but in his own way, treating his competitors with consideration, making their failures acceptable financially and, more important, personally. Settlements were generous, and negotiations honorable; and when Watson got his way, he did so more often than not by persuading the other fellow that the outcome was to his benefit, often hiring him as well as buying him out.

Business was business, most people said then, even those who lost out. But Watson began to wonder. He was ambitious. With this big chance he became a man with the eyes of an Elijah; but with the growing excitement, the mounting tensions as he glimpsed the heights ahead, there came, too, a desire to change the way the game was played. He was no reformer then. He was in no position to be — business, like politics, being a matter of the possible. But his subsequent career suggests that, although he may have wanted to forget the secondhand business entirely, he never did. Because he could not, he and American business in general would be the better for it.

At first, he moved to a new city every few months, but once he had the situation in the East under control, he settled in Chicago, making that his headquarters for operations extending from New York City to San Francisco. In the beginning, to his friends in the NCR he appeared as a competitor, but by 1906 Watson and his men were no longer hiding their connection with the National Cash Register Company in their negotiations. Finally, in February, 1907, the game was over, and the NCR announced that Thomas J. Watson was in charge of the secondhand business of the company. By then he had fifty-six employees, more than were in many of the sales districts.

Watson moved to Dayton, arriving as a promising young

executive who had made his way to the top, in a sense, from the outside, as free from embarrassing entanglements within the upper hierarchy as a man in the NCR could be, free, that is, from all but the friendship of Chalmers. Within a short time, that friendship threatened to end his career.

Watson arrived in time to see Dayton embroiled in civil war, the center of the battle none other than John H. Patterson. It was a fight that would rage, now and then, for eight years and have a far-reaching effect on his career. It would, in fact, be one of the crucial experiences of his life; but when it began, he was no more than a spectator.

Patterson had recently returned from a trip abroad to find that certain civic improvements needed by the company were being withheld, the reason, according to prevalent rumor, being corrupt local politicians. Patterson's conviction was that government was a business, no place for politicians, and for over ten years he had been urging local reforms including the adoption of a city manager. He was, as Watson said, a man "so far ahead of his time that people laughed at him and said he was crazy." Patterson shrugged off his neighbors' ridicule as ignorance and did what he could by himself, for example, operating his estate as a public park when the city refused to accept it as a gift. But, when public indifference struck at the welfare of his business, he took drastic action.

Early in March, 1907, less than a month after Watson moved into his new office, Patterson invited a thousand Dayton business leaders and clergymen to a meeting at the company's auditorium. At precisely the appointed hour he appeared on the platform, a crisp, dapper man, little over five and a half feet tall, dressed in black frock coat and striped trousers.

"Dayton is known now, and justly, too, I believe, as being the worst city in the state," Patterson began in his high-pitched voice, and then without the benefit of oratory he told the assemblage some plain truths. The people of the city were without ambition, the city was a malarial swamp, ugly and backward, and its leaders were corrupt. He named names and, so that there would be no misunderstanding, had pictures of the scoundrels flashed upon a huge screen while he detailed their misdoings. The NCR, he declared flatly, was considering moving to another city.

Three thousand citizens attended the next meeting, held a few days later; and Patterson aired more of his complaints, which boiled down to the fact that his company could not survive in a hostile community.

If young Watson was surprised at this close-up of his boss in action, the citizens of Dayton were aghast. The Dayton *Daily News* retaliated by publishing a heavy-handed satire of Patterson and the NCR entitled "The Glue Factory — Here to Stay, but Coax Us." Patterson, outraged, marked down as his enemy the editor, James M. Cox, a rising young Democratic politician. The city was still chuckling over his riposte when rains came; and, unhindered by the stanch levees that Patterson without success had urged upon the city, local rivers overflowed their banks and inundated the center of town. Patterson, who had wisely built his summer home on the terminal moraine to the south, with malicious calm held a party there for one thousand guests.

The fight began in earnest — on one side Cox, other local Democrats, and most of the one hundred and twenty thousand citizens of the town; on the other, Patterson and, for a time, the entire NCR. But finally the battle spread to the company itself, largely because of Patterson's evangelical enthusiasm in matters of health.

For years the old man had considered himself indestructible, if he considered himself at all, and, after the premature death of his wife, had lived a life of nothing but work. Finally, a few months after Watson took over the secondhand business, Patterson's health broke under the strain, and he went off to Europe to convalesce. There he fell into the hands of health faddists, one in particular — a small, wiry fellow five feet tall named Charles Palmer, a humorless man with a passion for the hard life. When Patterson recovered and returned to Dayton, Palmer came along as his personal servant, but before long he was a director of the company and czar in matters of health for cash register officials.

Patterson was convinced that what was good for him was mandatory for everyone else, and gradually the company took on the air of an athletic training camp as he permitted Palmer to institute his Spartan regime at headquarters. NCR officials, who had long before become accustomed to Patterson's taste for bottled water, his prejudice against pepper and butter, his enthusiasm for early hours and fresh air, now found themselves meeting more exacting requirements: calisthenics at dawn or long horseback rides through the wild Ohio countryside. The public considered the strange spectacle of a string of horses returning to the factory in the early morning hours, like a troop of Mosby's cavalry, and dubbed them the NCR Rough Riders, less in tribute to their endurance than in criticism of their style.

Patterson's interest in the welfare of his employees had begun back in the early days of the company when indifferent workman produced $50,000 worth of defective machines and almost ruined him. Patterson, in his usual direct manner, moved his desk into the factory, looked around him, and began making improvements. He built new factories flooded with sunlight and kept them spotless with white-coated attendants. He provided showers on company premises and company time, dining rooms with subsidized meals, entertainment, schools, clubs, libraries. His program was an investment, and it paid, he said gruffly whenever praised.

While reformers throughout the world applauded, there was unrest in Dayton. Patterson's benevolence proved insatiable, and so did Palmer's interference in business. With his hypnotic hold on the head of the company, Palmer was able to order executives about whether they were on horseback or not and, sizing up their business ability by his own mysterious brand of phrenology, give Patterson an excuse to fire those he had lost interest in. Finally, during the summer of the fight between Patterson and Dayton, Palmer intruded on the hitherto sacrosanct sales force, ordering that butter, bread, pepper, coffee, tea, and cigars be banned at the meeting of district sales managers. Someone had to put his foot down, and that someone was none other than Hugh Chalmers, the idol of the sales force, who had risen from office boy to vice-president, earning eighty thousand dollars a year and, he thought, the right to tell the president when he was wrong.

Patterson promptly fired him and, for good measure, a great number of his friends. Watson probably would have gone too; but Patterson, in looking over the records, discovered that he was making money, it was said more money than Chalmers with new machines.

"We should keep this man as he knows how to make money for us," Patterson is supposed to have commented.

Men wept when Chalmers left the factory, and the press whipped up a storm, claiming that Palmer was ruining the company and bringing Dayton low. There was a brief, sharp fight within the board of directors, but Patterson emerged victorious and, no doubt noting that there was a severe depression throughout the country, closed down the factory. He had to take the action, he said, to devote himself to the lawsuits with the press that had arisen from the Palmer affair.

Two thousand workers in the city were thrown out of work, and soon bread lines were forming in the streets. The NCR factory, its chimneys cold, was a silent rebuke to Patterson's detractors. As the impact of the old man's wrath was fully felt, sentiment changed, and Dayton turned its resentment on the newspapers which had stirred up the affair. Uneasily the *Daily News* defended itself, asking what the rights of a businessman were. "If he doesn't transact business according to the established custom of the community in which he lives — is that his private affair, which must be held to be sacred, and the newspapers denied the privilege of mention?"

After six months people had grown impatient with questions of paternalism and welfare-company jokes. Public meetings were held in tribute to Patterson, the other local newspapers scolded the *Daily News* for its calumnies, and the officers of the company signed a statement that "the simple rules of health and exercise which have been so often referred to and ridiculed, have been beneficial to us and of great value to the company." The workers in a mass meeting declared their gratitude to Patterson, one of the stirring speeches being given by a man who had broken his leg while riding a company horse.

Finally Patterson and Palmer left for Europe, and the factory was reopened. The lawsuits were settled out of court, and the company got its necessary civic improvements. Patterson did not move the factory to another city as he had threatened, but he did transfer the executive offices of the company to New York City.

The whole affair had a profound impact on Watson's career and on his thinking. In his conflict with Dayton, Patterson in many respects had been in the right. Much needed to be done to improve the city, and of his many suggestions for making Dayton a model community most would be adopted by the time he died, including the acceptance of a city manager. The trouble was that Patterson was immoderate even when right, and powerful even when wrong. He thought of his company as his personal affair; but even though he owned most of the stock, he was to find that his control could not be absolute. Because he was powerful, he thought he could afford enemies. Watson, though he, too, was a tempestuous man, knew this was not so, that business existed in a community and depended upon it. No business could afford to make enemies, within itself or without. Chalmers would one day make a great deal of trouble for John H. Patterson.

Patterson was a genius and, for the most part, brilliantly successful; but like most men of his kind, like Watson himself, he needed men around him who complemented him — balance wheels who could moderate and sometimes divert his enthusiasm, which were partly good, partly bad. One of the benefits to Patterson that arose out of the Palmer affair (and it was one with few benefits) was the acquisition of just such a man — Thomas John Watson, who in August, 1908, not long after Patterson left for Europe, was named assistant sales manager, in effect acting sales manager, for the general manager who succeeded Hugh Chalmers served as sales manager in name only, devoting himself to other matters in the company.

Probably no one was more surprised than Watson himself that arguments about railroad sidings and calisthenics had put him in the third most powerful seat in the NCR within a year of his arrival at headquarters. But there was far more to the sudden turn of events than Patterson's celebrated caprice. For several months, while Patterson battled the citizens of Dayton and his own officials, Watson with his secondhand business had been running the only money-making operation in the company. With the factory closed and production of new machines at a standstill, he found himself vaulted into prominence, a prominence dangerous in those days, considering Patterson's frame of mind and Watson's identification with Chalmers.

For a time survival was a matter of touch and go. One day during the fight, Watson arrived at work to find his staff gone and his office occupied by another executive, a kind of lockout Patterson used to presage a dismissal. Watson calmly went home. Every morning he returned to his office and, finding it still occupied, left without a word. When he met Patterson on the stairs, he nodded pleasantly and exchanged greetings, and he carried on his business from branch offices as if nothing had happened.

Finally Patterson, systematically banishing all traces of Chalmers' administration, put an end to the secondhand business as an independent operation. Watson's stores and personnel were disposed of or absorbed by the regular NCR offices, but instead of being fired, Watson, the money-maker, got his promotion and moved with other company executives to New York City.

At thirty-three he had achieved the uneasy summit of power in his company, and for two years he would exercise it almost entirely on his own, with little interference from other members of the hierarchy and none from Patterson, who was traveling about Europe, attending social functions "high up amongst the first aristocracy," he said.

Watson took his position at a difficult time, a time

when it was hard to persuade his salesmen that, having sold one hundred imperishable cash registers one year, they could the next. The theory of an expanding economy, the vision of the market place as an infinitely large, beckoning, endless expanse had yet to take hold of the American imagination. Darwin's assertion that warfare was the law of life was one that no salesman, with his daily struggle for survival, could have found remarkable. The theory of the survival of the fittest may have given comfort to those who were successful, but three serious depressions in the previous fifteen years had persuaded most of them that the economic world was small and that the fit would be few indeed.

Patterson's answer to this pessimistic view of affairs was simple and direct. The only limit to sales is the salesman, he believed. Equipped with enthusiasm and a few simple techniques, encouraged by an occasional sharp prod, he was to lead mankind — and the economy — upward and onward forever.

To fortify this argument was the brilliant record of Patterson's own company. In the first place, it had overcome public indifference to its product. (Back in the nineties, business as usual was business without cash registers, and it was up to Patterson and his men to make it otherwise, a feat accomplished under the baleful eyes of clerks called into line by "Ritty's Incorruptible Cashier," as it was originally known.) In the second place, the company had steadily grown bigger and better, successfully riding out the ebbs and flows of the economy, largely because of John H. Patterson's sales methods.

There was no doubt about it: Patterson was the father of modern salesmanship, the Henry Ford of distribution, who, by making mass selling possible, made mass production practical. It might be, as his detractors claimed, that he originated little, that most of his techniques had been used somewhere, at some time, by someone else; but even conceding that doubtful point, no one could deny that he was original in selecting what was effective and then applying it with ferocious energy and system. His conventions and schools, the quota system and the guaranteed territory, commissions and advances — this bag of tricks was his greatest contribution to American business, far greater than the machine he made famous.

Salesmanship, in Patterson's mind, boiled down to three matters: motivation, education, and technique.

As for motivation, he believed that all men act out of fear of punishment or hope of reward. The supreme punishment in business being dismissal, Patterson kept that fateful possibility conspicuously before his organization with a big turnover in personnel, striking down with impartial finality both the meek and mighty, as Chalmers learned. It was true that proximity to the old man, as well as being more rewarding, was more dangerous than distance, but distance from the head office was not security. Supervision was one of Patterson's ten commandments, and the long arm of headquarters reached out each week into the territory to receive the agent's report, which was compared to other records, published, and distributed to other agents throughout the country.

Fear was a poor substitute for enthusiasm, and so Pat-

terson put his energies to making selling to the best interest of the salesman. Commissions were generous; and
Patterson, operating under the unheard-of theory that
spending money is the way to make money, did not fol-
low the general custom of cutting them down when a
salesman began to make a comfortable living. And he
roused his men with dissatisfaction, sending them off to
his New York tailor to get the hayseed off them, he said,
knowing that a glimpse of the good life was a far more
effective incentive than an occasional noisy firing.

He stirred them with enthusiasm at conventions, permitting a salesman, by nature gregarious, the pleasure
of camaraderie with his own kind; whereas, before the
institution of the guaranteed territory, salesmen had been
forced to view their fellows, particularly those from their
own company, as pirates who would enrich themselves
by reaching into their own pockets. Between conventions
Patterson encouraged the team spirit with a lively, read-
able house organ.

And, knowing that a salesman is no better than the rest
of mankind, that there is, after all, a bit of pirate in his
heart, he turned that aggressive, competitive part of his
nature to the company's use, encouraging it with intracompany sales contests, rewarding the victorious with all
the satisfying visible signs of success — diamond stickpins
and gold-headed canes or, better still, promotion. Like
Watson, anyone in the NCR could rise to power overnight, and former office boys who sat on the board of
directors kept that bright promise alive in everyone's mind.

Along with enthusiasm, Patterson believed in training.

On the question of whether salesmen were born or made he refused a hard and fast judgment, saying only, "This training does not make salesmen. No training can do that." But with a nod toward native ability, he put his faith in education. He was, in fact, the originator of corporate schools, having started them in his company back in the early days long before Watson joined the NCR.

Company schools, however, did not mean that the cash register business was a place for pedants. Patterson's degree from Dartmouth had taught him a perverse contempt for the liberal arts and scholarship; and just as he was prejudiced in favor of youth, he preferred men who had a farm background to college graduates. Depending, as one of his men said, "on the practical teaching that a practical man gives to a group of well-selected practical men in front of him," Patterson was a pragmatist, the John Dewey of the business world, and the Pestalozzi as well. In his schools men were taught by other salesmen techniques that could not make a salesman, but made good dividends when used by the right man.

The matter of technique was an issue, one of the few, on which Watson differed with Patterson. When he took over his new job, he found himself at the head of the most creative and effective sales organization in America, but there was, he felt, room for improvement. Coming from the field force, with years of selling experience, Watson had a strong mistrust of theories about selling, even Patterson's theories, no matter how simple and direct they were. He knew that the primer had not brought about his own success at selling cash registers. He had needed the help of Jack Range, with his lightning intuition and spontaneity, to make a sale. Patterson with his schools and standard approach had imposed a much-needed order on free-wheeling drummers like Barron; but in his zeal for system he had gone too far, in Watson's opinion, restricting a man's individuality, which would remain, no matter how elaborate his training, his greatest asset as a salesman. It was to be Watson's role to loosen the ties on the sales force, to save order but resurrect liberty – in sum, to take the staginess out of the NCR salesman.

Matters had gone quite far when he got a hand in the matter. The primer was over twenty years old by the time Watson became acting sales manager; and although it had been revised over the years, had, in fact, been simplified the year before, it was in many ways obsolete in manner as well as theory. Watson did not eliminate the standard approach; no one in a company run by an autocrat like John H. Patterson ever turned a sharp corner in matters of policy. But he changed it. He outlined rather than detailed the demonstration, suggested arguments rather than prescribing them. Watson brought selling back to fundamentals – the straightforward approach of "go out and sell, go out and work."

"Never attempt to copy the manners and style of another," was the new and welcome order.

The credit for these revisions Watson shared with Joe Rogers, an expatriate Canadian who had been an NCR salesman in Utica when he was in Rochester. Rogers eventually became a special company representative but was not very prominent until Watson checked over his record and found it better than a dozen men combined. Watson made Rogers his assistant, and he was to become his greatest friend in business, serving as his complement as he was Patterson's.

In the matter of imparting dignity to the trade Watson and Rogers had no quarrel with Patterson. Watson himself always looked back with nostalgia to the era of the salesman in the tall silk hat; but with the industrialization that shook society in the nineties, both he and the country drummer like Cornwell had become obsolete. The new salesman like Barron, unsure of his place in the scheme of things, had shown a tendency to debase the calling, now no longer a rural treat like the county fair or a high-class exchange of merchandise over coffee and brandy.

Patterson had done what he could to put matters straight. His aim, and Watson's too, was to exalt the salesman, to restore his self-respect, to make a businessman out of him. Patterson likened the profession to that of a teacher. Watson did, too, and he liked telling the story of a minister in Meadville, Pennsylvania, who told a congregation of commercial travelers, in Watson's words, "Well, boys, I'm glad to be here with you. I'm only one of the boys. We're all engaged in the same kind of work."

With their high estimate of salesmanship Patterson and Watson infused their men with earnestness. In the place of the jolly promoter, with greasy vest, fat cigar, and belly laugh, they put a man who had been warned against familiarity and humor. "Put your trust in earnestness, candor and facts," he was enjoined. "There is nothing

the NCR had sold half a million cash registers, and in the next two, 1906–1908, the company sold another hundred thousand. Watson promptly doubled that record, bringing sales to more than one hundred thousand cash registers a year by 1910. Patterson rewarded him by making him sales manager in name as well as in fact. The date was May 28, 1910, eighteen years to the month from the time he began making his way in the world.

In June of the next year, the company with great fanfare shipped its millionth cash register, one-third of which number had been sold after 1907. Watson had to share some of the credit for the company's growth with a lanky country boy named Charles Kettering, who had put an electric motor on the machine at about the time Watson became assistant sales manager.

And now, he was to find, he had to share command with John H. Patterson.

Patterson had returned to Dayton early in 1910, bringing his executives back from New York City with him. During his years abroad, Patterson was often accused of neglecting his business, and occasionally the NCR in its official publications felt called upon to come to his defense, declaring that despite his absence he was taking a greater interest in company affairs than ever before. At no time, however, did Patterson feel a need to defend himself, his attitude being that travel was useful, that by putting distance between himself and his problems, he gained perspective. His country home in Dayton, Far Hills, served the same purpose, situated as it was upon a hill overlooking the factory. It represented his need for a rhythm of involvement and withdrawal in business, just as horseback riding did. Riding was healthful, just as travel was entertaining and educational, but mainly both afforded Patterson opportunities to think about business without distraction.

Once he was back in Dayton, there was no question about who was running affairs. Watson found himself face to face with one of the most interesting men to work for in America. He may have enjoyed the freedom he had when Patterson was in Europe, but he needed the experience that only the old man, tyrannical and unpredictable as he was, could give him in person.

Patterson, he found, was not easy to work for; but Watson, himself an impatient, demanding man, did it successfully as few men before or after him were able to. Patterson had no time for nonsense and oratory, and Watson learned to express himself crisply, in the NCR fashion — on an easel, in terse outline, breaking every problem, no matter what it was, into five parts. He shared Patterson's passion for work and the capacity to do it, day after day, from morning until night. He even shared Patterson's inclination to do much of his work away from his office. Physically lazy, Watson preferred to sit and think without the distraction of a horse, although he was a good rider. Often when a friend stopped by to drive him to work, Watson would call him in, stir up his fire, lean back in his chair and, lighting up a cigar, settle down to talk about business until noon before he got up to go to his office. But whenever Patterson came down the hall of the executive building looking for someone to ride with him, Watson was always willing and often chosen.

In time Watson developed an instinct for understanding the incalculable John Patterson. He sensed when suggestions could be made, when a tribute from the sales force would be appreciated, when it was possible to make changes in the boss's favorite project, and when it was prudent to be invisible. Above all, Watson had an insight of profound importance for the company as a whole — that executives, as well as salesmen, liked appreciation, that Patterson needed loyalty as much as the NCR needed him as the focus of its enthusiasm.

When Patterson returned from Europe, the company was in desperate need of consolidation. During the Chalmers fight, district managers had been handed many of the powers of central management, and with decentralization had come disunity and confusion. Company gatherings, once a common practice, lapsed. His greatest handicap during Patterson's absence, Watson felt, was not having meetings with the executives under him. Now, to re-establish morale and order in the company, he and Patterson began traveling around the country together, holding meetings in St. Louis, New York, and Chicago. And Watson reinstituted the company practice of having frequent conventions in Dayton with the declared object of introducing the men to their president, who had been gone so long that many, even important executives, did not know him.

Patterson had begun the practice of holding conventions years before, shortly after he took over the company. Starting as a caucus of five, they had grown as the company and Patterson's enthusiasm grew until they acquired a peculiar grandeur — part circus, part camp meeting, part Chautau-

qua. There were conventions for all of the company salesmen at which bands played, flags flew in the gusty Ohio
winds, and men were exhorted to work and to love their
work and to know how to work. The chief NCR meetings
were not these, however, but the Hundred Point clubs,
conventions for salesmen who had made 100 per cent or
better of their quota for the year, a minimum of thirty
thousand dollars' worth of business. By the time Patterson
returned from Europe, about two hundred salesmen quali-
fied for this big show — a trip to Dayton, all expenses
paid, for several days of honor and majesty, band music
and speeches, and a good time with the boys.

There was about these affairs, as viewed long afterward, the air of a sober Victorian musical. The men,
arriving on special trains in the dead of winter, were met
at the station by an official delegation and escorted to the
factory, one year in sleds, the next in special sight-seeing
cars, curious vehicles with rows of seats on an airy platform behind the driver. They were given trips through the
factory, where they had their annual look at disemboweled
machines and their annual admonition to ignore, for pur-
poses other than curiosity, the mystery of their parts. They
sat through meetings in swivel chairs and adjourned, will-
ingly after the long day, to the Officers Club, a proud
building with paneled walls and leather sofas, for a game
of checkers or jokes about life in the territory. Banquets
were held at a huge horseshoe table at the Officers Club,
where the men were served by waiters in glistening white
uniforms. The antiseptic mood suggested by mashed vege-
tables and bottled water was dispelled by the manly air of

patriotism and worldliness evoked by the flags and national shields which Patterson invariably selected as decorations. In the evenings the men gathered in their Spartan bedrooms, furnished with generous water bowls and iron bedsteads. There they smoked and talked, sitting easily on their beds as men accustomed to the road, their bowlers and umbrellas on their trunks beside them.

They posed for pictures — the inevitable mass photograph of the entire force shivering on the plain before the factory, rising behind them in a surprising display of enterprise and enlightenment, concrete testimony to Patterson's vision. The general portrait was a chilling tradition that Patterson alone set great store by, but the men obviously enjoyed posing with the other salesmen in their district — all immaculate and proud, with the flush of men just emerged from the shower, boutonnieres in their lapels, in their hands the little leather bags containing their monetary reward for merit.

Besides providing an obvious opportunity for rewarding good works, these conventions were educational, in Watson's view. "This is not a convention, it is a school," he told one meeting. Patterson, too, took this attitude and, incidentally, made the meetings the occasion for fervent missionary work in the field of health, in which he had lost no interest despite ridding himself of Palmer sometime during his stay in Europe. Watson himself preached the advantages of good health, but did not go to extremes as one executive did, informing salesmen that "there is a direct relation between your liver and the sale of cash registers."

But even more important than the information exchanged, the speeches on selling points and company policy, was the effect of conventions on morale. They unified the far-flung company, bound it into a family with the factory serving as home and the officers as the center of loyalty. The sales convention was Patterson's — and Watson's — solution of the problem of the national company, a way of maintaining unity as the NCR stretched to the far corners of the country, of keeping up a small-company spirit along with big-company organization and dividends.

Watson was at his best at these meetings. Never an orator, he was, nevertheless, a good speaker and popular with the men. In the Officers Club, sitting around with the boys, smoking a cigar, he was a good fellow like the rest, relaxed, casual, always ready with a practical joke. But when he was at the right hand of Patterson, he was another man entirely, and his face, in moments when he was caught off guard, had the drawn, strained air that was to dominate it for the next forty years. In group pictures, no matter how large, Watson's was the most striking face. Still handsome, somewhere between youth and age he was, with eyes that burned from the page. His coarse, straight black hair and lean face reminded men of a handsome Lincoln, and he dressed well, very well in a conservative way, his only jewelry being a stickpin in his tie.

Most of the salesmen looked like salesmen, a few of the executives, like executives. John H. Patterson alone looked like a corporation president, and Thomas John Watson, his most attentive student, had already begun to look like him — the same concentrated force flaring in his eyes, the same distinction in his manner. They were different in ways that were fundamental to be sure; but their similarities were important and especially striking as they emerged.

In his meddling, thoughtful way John H. Patterson took a great interest in Watson's development. He once called on him at his hotel, the best in Dayton, looked his quarters over, and said, "I don't think this is the address you ought to have. I'm going to build you a house." He did, and Watson was not permitted to pay rent, no matter how much he protested. And Patterson bought him a car, the Pierce-Arrow that Watson had for years.

But for all his kindnesses Patterson was a harsh man to work for, and a dangerous one, too. For one thing, he was majestically inconsistent. Once when Watson pointed out a contradiction in orders, Patterson snapped, "There are only two kinds of people who don't change their minds — fools and dead people." And he was exacting and critical. He criticized, Patterson explained to Watson, because he was Watson's friend. Friends criticize when things go wrong, he said, but enemies say nothing, hoping they can profit by mistakes.

Gradually, as he observed Patterson, Watson began to understand some of his techniques of management, to see the theory of punishment and reward at work — and to put it to work for himself. In time he gained a reputation for being touchy, and many people in the company became afraid of him. The motto of one of his favorite salesmen was "Get out, or get in line," a harsh injunction, but, Watson began to feel, a necessary one in business. He often told a story about one of his men who, when promoted, told his salesmen, "I want you to remember that if you men do not do your job properly, you are going to interfere with my success as district manager, or possibly something bigger."

But Watson was respected and well liked because he was fair. He might scold a man who disobeyed an important policy in an emergency, but he would double his salary at the same time, saying, "You'd rather break a rule than break the company."

Watson took few vacations during those years; and when he did, he would soon return despite assurances from Patterson that everything was going well at Dayton. ("It has been a long time since you have had a vacation, and you need it, and you needed it long ago, and resist the temptation of coming back before you are entirely recovered," Patterson would tell him.) But Watson was restless. He would leave the resorts and spas, "only intended for sick people," and hurry back to his desk. He had had some insight into what he could accomplish, and he had decided, as he confided to one of his friends, that someday he would be one of the greatest businessmen in America.

3

THE TRIAL

ABSORBED in his work, Watson had no more time for a private life than he had for vacations. His position in the NCR had brought him prominence in Dayton society, where he made his way with ease and pleasure — a popular bachelor, good dancer, member of all the prominent clubs. He played some golf, helped organize the annual horse show, tinkered with automobiles. But his real recreation was business, and after a long day at the office he often sat up most of the night, talking about the trade with another company officer or any of the sales agents who happened to be in town — Jack Range or Pliney Eves or one of the Laird brothers.

In those years his closest friend, besides Joe Rogers, was his roommate, the scholarly John Hayward, one of the NCR patent attorneys. Hayward, with his pedantic air, his philosophic, speculative mind, was a piece of eighteenth-century Boston transplanted to the flatlands of Ohio. Watson was drawn to friends like him, men who were his opposites in temperament and background, perhaps partly because he felt that he had something to learn from them. Hayward, a former Harvard professor, introduced him to literature, poetry, and music and was amazed at the man's capacity to learn, for he rarely opened a book. Watson, in turn, taught Hayward how to ride, a skill helpful in those days for an executive career in the National Cash Register Company.

They lived in various places, hotels like the Belle Clair in New York or the houses Patterson provided for his officials in Dayton at Hills and Dales, the company country club. Loving motion for its own sake, as he did, Watson did not mind shifting about from one place to another. Whatever need for stability he had was fulfilled by his family. In the decade after he left home, his devotion to his mother and sisters, instead of fading, had grown, giving him roots that were indestructible, so that he could live happily anywhere, in hotel room or boardinghouse, knowing that he had after all, a home and family that were his.

Despite his long absences from Rochester he remained undisputed head of the household, with great stature even in the families of his sisters, two of whom had married company salesmen. Watson was especially close to his mother, a remarkable, regal-looking old woman, well educated for her time and religious, with a firm sense of right and wrong. Every month Watson journeyed to Rochester to visit her, no matter how busy he was. He took her to company dinners and sent her expensive presents like a piano and an electric car. Once when she was ill, he sent her a package of presents, one to be opened each day of her convalescence.

For years he helped support her generously and, his mother thought, at times extravagantly. He wanted her to have all the luxuries he could now afford, but her harsh, frugal life had not prepared her to enjoy them. Watson once invited her to stay at the Waldorf Hotel in New York and in the morning suggested they have breakfast in her room. She ordered some milk.

Didn't she want something else? Watson asked.

What? With coffee thirty-five cents a cup? she asked indignantly.

As Watson neared forty, his mother became anxious for him to marry. He had always liked women and been popular with them; and in his early years in Buffalo and Rochester, his sisters had teased him about his many girl friends, saying they could always determine his current favorite by giving his horse its head, letting him amble off to the right house. Watson had been engaged twice, once to a singer from Philadelphia who refused to give up her career for marriage and thereby ended the affair. The other girl had a bad temper, as Watson discovered one day when he arrived unannounced at her door and overheard her quarreling with her mother. He may have decided that one temper in a family was enough. At any rate, he broke off his engagement and, whatever his reasons were, kept them to himself, leaving the girl without an explanation.

In the years afterward Watson, having glimpsed the possibility of success, threw all his energies into making his way to the top of the NCR pyramid. He was patient about the matter of a wife as he was patient about nothing else in his life. He would wait for the right time, when he could marry a woman he would always be proud of, a member of one of the first families of Dayton.

He met Jeannette Kittredge late in the spring of 1912 at a party at one of the local country clubs. Her parents were Presbyterians, strict leaders of the church, and no one in the family drank. That day the young woman noticed that only one other wineglass at the table was left untouched. It was Watson's, she saw. She had caught a glimpse of him once before when attending a concert with John Hayward. Now she decided that she would like to meet him. Watson, too, observed that someone besides himself was not drinking and determined to meet her.

It is curious that their relationship began in this way. In many respects the incident reveals them both sharply — strong-willed, upright, uncompromising, living as they chose, regardless of what others did. But the mood of the meeting, the element of negation, was uncharacteristic. The relationship that began with the untouched wineglasses was to be one of the most assertive and positive marriages of its time.

Jeannette Kittredge was twenty-nine, a beautiful young woman with soft eyes and a shy manner that made her seem younger than she was. There was some Quaker blood in her background and a great deal of New England, but her father was an Ohioan, a very successful businessman, at one time president of the Barney and Smith Railroad Car Company of Dayton. At sixteen she had left home to go to college, first attending Wooster, later Wheaton Seminary in Massachusetts. Then she returned to Dayton to live with her family in their large town house on Ludlow Street, across from that of John H. Patterson.

When Watson told the old man of their engagement, Patterson said with satisfaction, "I was hoping you would marry that girl."

For a long time the engagement was kept secret. The reason may have been that by the end of that year Watson was involved in a court case that threatened to send him to jail.

The matter went back to the fateful dismissal of Hugh Chalmers that had rocked the National Cash Register Company not long after Watson first came to Dayton. When he was fired, Chalmers strode off to Detroit to take over the Thomas Detroit Company, in time becoming the first super-salesman of the automobile industry. But he was troubled from the very beginning by thoughts of revenge: Watson knew of the rumor that, when he left, Chalmers had told Patterson he would ruin him with a cheap cash register. The NRC tried through the courts to enjoin Chalmers and his friends from carrying off their know-how to competitors, but despite Patterson's efforts those men threw in their lot with other cash register companies, and the battle began. Chalmers was confident that he could beat the NCR organization, feeling that Patterson got far too much credit for the success of the company, and his balance wheels, namely himself, far too little.

Competition, almost nonexistent for several years, suddenly picked up. Sensing litigation in the wind, Watson tried without success to keep abreast of events. Across his desk streamed confidential reports on the fight being waged in the field; and, although the tales he heard were often unreliable, it was clear that both sides were resorting to questionable tactics under duress.

The fight came to a head late in the fall of 1910 when American Cash Register salesmen began giving depositions to a state court in Detroit, charging the NCR with unfair competition against their company. The American company was successor to the Hallwood Cash Register Company, which had given Watson trouble back in Rochester. It had finally gone bankrupt, only to take on renewed life and another name when Chalmers and his friends put their talents to work there.

When the case came to trial, Watson found himself at the center of the controversy.

The story that unfolded was by no means clear. The trouble had begun the year before, in 1909, when a star NCR salesman in Detroit resigned to take over the American Cash Register agency in that city. He was an old-timer with an outstanding sales record, and his defection to the other side was a matter of first importance, calling for the appearance of Watson as acting sales manager at the installation of his successor, Watson's close friend George Lingham.

What happened on that occasion was a matter of spirited debate during the trial, with the men who had attended the meeting unable to agree on the time, location, and speakers, much less on what was said. The chief witnesses for the prosecution claimed that Watson outlined a campaign of sharp practices designed to put them out of business. Witnesses for the defense contended, on the other hand, that Watson had urged his men to look upon competition as a good thing.

"He said it was just like a dog having fleas," testified one. "If he didn't have enough of them, he wouldn't know he was a dog."

There were similar discrepancies in the testimony on every other major point before the court. The American Cash Register salesmen charged that, after Lingham took over the NCR office, their salesmen and customers were harassed, their men pirated, their cash register undersold by an NCR machine specially priced for competition. In a short time the company was forced to close its Detroit office. NCR men, on the other hand, claimed that the American Cash Register Company had pirated its men, put spies in its office, and had stolen lists of prospective customers. The judge in the case probably shook his head in disbelief as he heard how the battle often ended with a fist fight in a customer's store.

Watson undoubtedly grimaced. It was true that he had presided over the much-disputed meeting in Detroit and outlined a program to meet the competition there, had even assigned specially trained "competition men" to that territory. But, although the extent of his responsibility for what occurred afterward was in doubt, it was clear that he did not countenance the boisterous free-swinging salesman there, or anywhere else for that matter. Favor him or not, Watson was implicated as company practices, long the subject of debate within the NCR, came under the scrutiny of the public and the courts.

While the Michigan case was still pending, the NCR got embroiled in more serious trouble in Ohio. On February 22, 1912, John H. Patterson and twenty-nine other officials of the National Cash Register Company were indicted by the Federal Court for the Southern District of Ohio for violation of the Sherman Antitrust Act. Watson was one of the men who was to stand trial.

Whatever part Ohio politics had played in the indictment, it was clear that the trump card had come from Washington. The Republican administration was approaching the Presidential elections with a startling flurry of activity on the part of the Attorney-General, George W. Wickersham. Securing President Taft's name as a trust-buster, he filed antitrust suits at an unprecedented rate for a total of ninety, more than twice as many as were instituted by the previous administration. The *New York Times* commented that the NCR case put "the administration of the law on trial as truly as the trust defendants. . . . Is it not about time that the antitrust laws should be enforced for reasons of public interest rather than for political objects?"

Shocked NCR officials saw the issue in personal terms: the Attorney-General had once been a lawyer for a company now run by Hugh Chalmers; the prosecuting attorney was the President's brother-in-law; the judge in the case had a friend who had lost money in a competitive cash register company and was himself reported to be outspokenly bitter against the NCR. Most serious of all was

the fact that the officials were being tried under the criminal provisions of the law. If they were found guilty, they
might have to serve jail sentences.

By 1912 the National Cash Register Company was
thought to control over 90 per cent of the cash register
business. But the theory that bigness itself was illegal had
not as yet evolved in the judicial interpretations of the
Sherman Antitrust Act, and the charges against the NCR
were not based on the size of the company. The question
at issue was the methods of the company. The statute of
limitations under the criminal provisions of the law was
three years, but the prosecution was permitted to attempt
to prove that for twenty years the company used "unfair,
oppressive, tortuous, illegal and unlawful means" to dis-
courage competition. It was not difficult for the government to substantiate many damaging charges against the
company, which had made its way for almost a decade in
a world largely uninstructed by the slowly evolving moral
conscience that was given form, but not entire substance,
with the passage of the Sherman Act in 1890. Afterward,
to be sure, some of the company practices continued,
according to the laws of social inertia and Patterson's
conviction that the field was his and that marauders had,
therefore, better beware.

"It was said of him, with apparent fidelity, that he
thought himself divinely appointed to make cash registers,"
said one wit. In Patterson's mind the case was less ecclesi-
astical than legal, purely a business matter, based on patents
and hard work. He was a man who liked short words, but

he was not given to understatement; and during the trial he was much quoted. The effect was damaging, especially when the court directed its attention to his uninhibited remarks of the early days.

"We do not buy out," he had thundered. "We knock out!"

"If you are going to kill a dog," he used to say in defense of his methods, "it would be much kinder to hit him on the head instead of beginning with his tail and cutting off an inch or two at a time."

At the time of the trial Patterson's proprietary attitude still prevailed in the company. A salesman, writing to Watson, summed it all up by saying, "It would seem therefore to right-minded people that having created this business, President Patterson is entitled to all of it, and the laws of the country should prevent thieves from breaking in and taking that which does not belong to them, rather than encourage them to do so."

Watson, it should be noted, did not answer.

The four main witnesses for the prosecution were Hugh Chalmers, two of the officials who left the NCR with him, and the former NCR salesman who had been the center of the court fight in Detroit. They were the ones who supplied company correspondence about competition, and they were the ones who produced firsthand testimony about opinion and strategy in the high councils of the company. It was not surprising, considering the fact that they themselves were implicated in the damaging charges they advanced, that the testimony was often hazy, the witnesses hurried. What is surprising is that they appeared at all. The three-year statute of limitations ensured that they would escape jail, all having left the NCR before the critical period; but their testimony put their integrity in serious jeopardy. Chalmers had been general manager for four and a half years before leaving the NCR; both of the other officials were on the now notorious competition committee of the company; and the three of them freely involved themselves in the decisions and practices being detailed to prove illegal conspiracy.

Watson, in seeking their motives, must have been forced to conclude that bitterness alone was the answer. He had heard many times that Chalmers had boasted, "I will not be even with the old man till I put him behind bars." Apparently, then, revenge was to be sweeter than a good name.

As competitive policies of the NCR were detailed by the gleeful company traitors, the prosecuting attorney's indignation blazed, and he declared at one point that the methods "find no parallel in civilized business methods; they might, perhaps, find an echo in the methods of the bandits of Mexico. . . ." There were the expected charges of pirating salesmen, of bribery and spying and sabotage, of pay-offs in dark places and secret deals in back rooms. Eventually the whole scope of the company's campaign against competition was exposed: patent litigation and other legal harassment of rivals; the production of special machines called Knockers, selectively marketed, often at a loss, to overcome any threat of competition; the special salesmen or Knockout Men, as they were called, specially

trained to meet competition, operating in the patient, pains-
taking manner of salaried men, not worried about commissions, with broad company interests in mind, orders from
above, and few people to answer to. The company practice
of displaying defective machines of competitors promi-
nently with disparaging comment was noted, as was the
famous graveyard of rusty cash registers of defunct companies that was long part of the Dayton scene. The Gloom
Room, sometimes known as the Historical Room, came
under scrutiny and turned out to be a factory display, maintained to dishearten visitors with an interest in producing
rival cash registers by showing them examples of machines
that failed with a summary of how much money was lost in
the ventures. Watson later claimed that he saw two hundred and fifty other cash register companies come and go
during his years with the NCR; and, although he may have
exaggerated the number, he was right about the fate of
competitors. By the end of 1912 there were only three rival
companies, none of them in good condition.

Watson knew that some of the charges against the company were true from the investigations he had made during the Michigan case. Although he could hardly be held
responsible for business practices at the turn of the century, as acting head of the sales department and a director
of the company, he was partly responsible for current
policy. Furthermore, he was personally implicated by some
of the testimony. The Detroit affair was taken as a case study
to prove that the strong-arm methods of the 1890's had
been used by the NCR in recent years. Even though a case
against the company loomed up in the murky testimony,

Watson's own part was in question, there being no proof that he had ordered the doubtful practices. More embarrassing to him was the secret secondhand business, which Chalmers and his friends discussed in stubborn detail.

Less clear was his role as sales manager in the company's over-all campaign against competition. He was accused of ordering his men to report to Dayton on the activities of other companies in the field and of having charge of a few of the special competition men like Jack Range, also a defendant. But much of the company correspondence introduced to show Watson's complicity in the alleged conspiracy consisted of letters bearing Watson's signature, but dictated by one of his associates, who signed the letters also, indicating that the authority was not Watson's, or of letters signed with a rubber stamp, indicating that they did not have Watson's personal attention, indeed, that he may not have known of them at all.

Watson was known to be tough on competition, but he was also known to have opposed many of the questionable policies, contending that eventually they would injure the company's name and affect its balance sheet. The fact that practices had changed a great deal in the last three years, during the time when Watson had considerable authority, was discounted by the government, which charged that by that time most of the competition was already destroyed. And the chief basis for the NCR's defense was swept away by the presiding judge, who ruled out any evidence showing that competitors had infringed patents of the NCR, thereby preventing the company from arguing that the rascals got what they deserved.

It seemed, Watson concluded, that the judge's action was equivalent to his saying to the NCR, when the company rose to begin its defense, "I adjourn the court."

As the trial dragged on, the defendants began to show signs of strain. By Christmas, friends were confidently linking Watson's name with Jeannette Kittredge's; and the company, despite the preoccupation of its chief officers, had its best January in history, but these events only seemed to heighten Watson's anxiety, as if he were seeing plainly, once and for all, what was at stake in the Federal court. Hayward, also named in the indictment, was confident that a conviction would not hold up in a court of appeals because of the judge's ruling about evidence. Watson was afraid he might be wrong, and eventually, to the annoyance of some of the other defendants, he brought in one of the leading attorneys in the country, John B. Stanchfield, to act as his personal lawyer and help advise the NCR.

At 10:30 on the morning of February 13, 1913, company officials were notified that a verdict had been reached. The foreman of the jury arose and pronounced the fateful words: all but one had been found guilty, and that one was not Watson. Patterson's children wept on his shoulder, and the city of Dayton gave a cry of shock and pain. The fact of dependence on the NCR, so clearly demonstrated during the months of conflict after Chalmers' departure, had evoked much loyalty to the company in its home city; and, when the defendants were given heavy jail sentences, the city was stunned.

Facing the judge for the final time, the defendants

heard him bitterly score the company for its business practices. "You men belong to the walk of life which should
set the example," he said. "Yet you have lost the opportunity given you by the methods you pursued. In your
desire for gain you forgot everything else." Watson and
Joe Rogers, along with Patterson, got the maximum sentence — a year in jail.

The outcome was widely debated, every businessman
feeling that the issues of the case were his own concern.
Most major newspapers favored the conviction, although
many criticized the harshness of the sentence, holding that in
view of the general disregard of the antitrust laws it was
unfair to make the NCR an example. Only one previous
prosecution under the Sherman Act had resulted in jail
sentences — that against three officers of the turpentine
trust who were even then appealing their case to the
Supreme Court.

The reaction in the NCR varied. One salesman said
grandly, "Our president, right or wrong, our president."

Another wryly told the story of two Scots traveling
across the ocean during a heavy storm. In panic one rushed
to the other crying that the boat was sinking.

"Well, what do you care?" said the other dourly. "You
don't own it."

Patterson's daughter wired flowers to the afflicted families, and local florists, misreading the occasion, in many
instances sent funeral wreaths.

Watson's friends hastened to console him. One assumed
a grating jocularity, saying, "Now that you are at last a real
genuine 'criminal,' your friends at Peekskill want to be

among the first to shake your 'guilty' hand and wish you joy or whatever the proper phrase is." An understanding friend said, "I know you are thinking more of your mother and sister than you are of yourself and I do hope they have not taken it too hard."

His friends in Painted Post, still working in the local stores, had watched with pride Watson's rise to the top of the NCR pyramid, saying without envy that his success was "only another illustration of what good old American grit and 'stick-to-itiveness' can accomplish." When the verdict was announced, they were shaken. Watson wrote to one of them asking that everyone be told that "while I am under jail sentence, I do not consider myself a criminal. . . . I am absolutely innocent of any conspiracy such as we have been charged with, and I can state truthfully, that I have not committed a single act during my career of seventeen years with the NCR Co., that I am, in the least ashamed of, or that I am not willing to have the whole world know about. . . ."

To another friend he wrote, "Of course, the announcements in the newspapers of the jail sentences are not the most pleasant things in the world to read, but I want to assure you and all my friends that I am not worried, in the least, about this matter; neither do I feel at all humiliated. My conscience is clear, and I am quietly awaiting the action of the Court of Appeals."

But it was not possible to maintain his self-possession before everyone. He went to Jeannette Kittredge and asked her, under the circumstances, to break their secret engagement. No, she said, now he would need her more than ever. She insisted that they announce their engagement immediately and be married in April, months before the Circuit Court of Appeals was to hand down its decision.

Watson knew that he had come to a turning point in his life, but then he had no way of knowing how much her faith in him would mean. The successful life he had built for himself in Dayton had received a blow, he thought, but it was, in fact, beginning to crumble. The years ahead would be difficult: at forty he would have to begin his life again. Without Jeannette Kittredge, without her strong confidence in him, it would have been difficult indeed.

Exhausted by the strain of the long trial, Watson wanted to get away from Ohio, away from the depressing March rains and probably, for the first time in his life, away from business. Shortly after the verdict was handed down, he went off to Philadelphia and then on to New York City, where Jeannette was shopping for her trousseau with her sister Helen and her mother.

On the evening of March 25 he had dinner with them and several other Daytonians at the Waldorf Hotel. John Hayward was there and Watson's young assistant Robert Houston. John H. Patterson probably would have been with them if it had not been for his constitution, as he called his little red notebooks in which he wrote inviolable thirty-day schedules of his affairs. He had come to New York on his way to see the President to present his side of the antitrust case, but his assistants had succeeded in preventing that hopeless venture; and Patterson, discovering in his current red book that he had promised to speak to the Dayton Boy Farmers' Club, one day abruptly got up from lunch with Hayward and Watson and returned to Ohio.

Within a few days he was a national hero. The train he took to Dayton was one of the last to reach the city for a long time. After the party at the Waldorf, Houston, by mysterious means known only to advertising men, heard the disturbing rumor that Dayton had been hit by a flood. Alarmed, he went to the offices of the *New York Times* to check the report, but in vain, for all communications with the city seemed to be cut off. The next morning the NCR office found that it had the only telegraph line still operating from Dayton. That city was in a state of chaos, possibly threatened with extinction.

Three days earlier, on March 23, a tornado had swept through the Midwest, but Dayton had been spared, and hundreds of people had braved ugly rains to attend Easter services at the local churches. The rain continued through that night, and water rose steadily behind the twenty-five-foot levees holding back the muddy Miami River and its two tributaries that met just north of town and there hooked to the east, flowing around the great flatlands that held the center of town. By Monday the water table had risen so far that the city seemed to float, an illuminated mirage in a great shallow lake. Finally, early Tuesday morning, March 25, the levees broke, and a wall of water roared south through the center of town, sweeping away buildings, destroying homes, imprisoning thousands. Fifteen square miles were covered with six to eighteen feet of water, but still the water rose and rushed through town with unabated force. During that night explosions rocked the city until a freezing rain brought an end to fires. When the dark morning came, efforts began to rescue the thousands of people huddled on roofs of buildings, in danger of being swept away by the force of the current. Ninety thousand people were homeless, and property damage was incalculable.

As the waters slowly began to recede, the dominant structure that came into view was John H. Patterson. James Cox, now Ohio's governor, named his former enemy virtual dictator of Dayton in recognition of the fact that Patterson commanded the only island of activity in the paralyzed city — the National Cash Register Company, standing intact on high ground south of town. Patterson, in his customary uninhabited manner, took advantage of his position to send out a sizzling telegram to his company's New York office to be relayed to the *New York Times* announcing that should the judge who presided in the antitrust hearings set his foot in the area under his jurisdiction, he would slap him in jail.

Watson was indignant that his boss should use that historic moment, when all the world waited for the first word from Dayton, for a message so characteristic and unpublishable. He tore it up, and forgetting Patterson's touchy feelings, fired back an order: no more telegrams except those dealing with the flood. Then, turning to reporters with manner as grave as the responsibilities the company now assumed, he and his assistants began outlining what the company was doing to meet the crisis, elaborating on the elliptical reports slowly coming over their wire, for three days Dayton's only link with the outside world.

Despite his telegram Patterson was behaving magnificently. The factory — its power, heat, electric, and water plants intact — became the center of rescue operations, the ark that was to carry the city through its greatest trial. Patterson turned over the complete facilities of the NCR to the people of the city, setting his workers to making boats, sending them out to bring people to safety and patrol accessible areas to prevent looting and violence. Thousands of people were fed in the company cafeteria, at first on rice and beans and later, as Patterson marshaled the resources of the countryside, on everything he could lay his hands on, without regard to price. A hospital was organized, and five babies were born at the factory on the first day. Thousands slept there every night, making their beds on hay that Patterson managed to obtain somewhere. It was changed every night; for Patterson, with glorious unconcern in the face of disaster, maintained his meticulous attention to matters of hygiene. Paper cups were mandatory, and people were provided with bottled water and clean dry clothes and ordered to drink malted milk and wear woolen stockings.

Once Patterson, in the interest of symmetry, had ordered two buildings moved within a week and, being told that the task was impossible, had it done overnight. Now in this same highhanded manner, he ordered his men to do the impossible — ship fifty cookstoves in from Cincinnati, get drinking water for one hundred and twenty thousand people, obtain forty new cars. When the impossible was accomplished, legends sprang up around him — that he was found at the end of a towline, waist-deep in the chill water, that he spent a million dollars of his company's money in a week and wrote it off as a business expense. The stories were but shadows of the central fact that John H. Patterson saved the city, first with the resources of his factory, then with his spirit. It is not surprising that he was able to infuse the disheartened city with a will to go on and rebuild. He had in his time defied everything from the people of Dayton to the laws of the land. A flood did not dismay him.

While Patterson played his heroic part in Dayton, Watson played his in New York. The National Cash Register Company was being offered a reprieve, a single golden chance to redeem itself; and Watson and his assistants fell to work to snatch their opportunity. Within a few hours after learning of the disaster they had equipped a relief train with desperately needed supplies — food, drugs, water, tents; and a few minutes after midnight on the morning of March 27 it started out for Dayton. Watson himself was in charge of arranging transportation, and it was said later that he practically built a railroad to Dayton, arranging for new switches to be put in and tracks to be relaid. Where he could not get the railroad repaired, he had to depend upon manpower, and many of the supplies he shipped from New York were carried by hand the last few miles into the city.

Before the first train had reached Cleveland, another was on its way with more food and medical supplies, as well as doctors and nurses. By Friday, March 28, the third and final NCR relief train, fitted out as a hospital, set out in the charge of John Hayward, its mission somewhat deflated by an unexpected telegram from Patterson, the only one arriving from Dayton that day, saying that no more medical help was necessary.

Exhausted, Watson was ordered off to a hospital, but by then the NCR had met the emergency with honor, and he knew that his friends could carry on. Everyone in the company had contributed to the efforts that lifted the cloud hanging over the NCR, but Watson himself had done more than most to produce the bright image of the company that now, thanks to the press, dominated the public mind.

While the NCR had the only communication with Dayton, the company office on lower Broadway had become a press center, where reporters came and went night and day. On the first train to leave New York for Dayton were more reporters, who upon arrival became guests of the NCR, making their headquarters on the top floor of the factory, where they were provided room and board, whisky and cards.

When Patterson, who was himself a teetotaler, went up to make sure they had proper accommodations, his embarrassed assistant explained that the men in the smoke-filled rooms were playing pinochle and drinking pop. Patterson, for once permitting himself to be deluded, said, "Oh, yes," and never went back. Thereafter reporters were left to themselves, free to observe the miracle of the NCR organization at work, the brightly lit factory, efficient teams of rescuers, the openhanded refuge. In the calamity of mud and water, millions of dollars of damaged property and thousands of homeless, a hero was clearly needed; and Patterson played the role with the same dramatic flare that he had once played devil. Only when old J. P. Morgan died a few days later did the NCR slip from the front pages of the papers throughout the country; but by then the entire nation had witnessed the curious spectacle of John H. Patterson, representing the civil authority of one of the largest cities in Ohio, conferring with the Secretary of the Army and the Army chief of staff about the maintenance of law and order while under jail sentence on a criminal charge.

"Little Eva" Booth, commander of the Salvation Army, addressing the multitude at the NCR during the height of the crisis, had praised Patterson, crying, "It is a noble work and will be rewarded by One who recognizes good deeds." Patterson's friends took action to see that he would have his earthly reward, sending a telegram to the newly inaugurated President Wilson asking that he be pardoned because of his work during the flood.

Patterson promptly sent another to the President saying, "I make haste to assure you that these messages and efforts are without my knowledge or consent. I am guilty of no crime. I want no pardon. I want only justice."

Patterson, with apparent indifference about his own fate, set to work raising money for the reconstruction of the city and a flood control project that eventually became the fifty-million-dollar Miami Conservancy District, but it was plain to everyone that the flood would leave its watermark on the antitrust proceedings, one way or another.

Watson and Jeannette Kittredge returned to the stricken city for their wedding. Neither wanted to postpone it, and so it took place as scheduled, little more than two weeks after the flood waters had receded. Necessarily, it was, as a local newspaper commented, "the most simple wedding recorded in society annals in Dayton in many seasons." The ceremony was held in the Kittredge town house, which had had four feet of water in it during the flood but was relatively undamaged. Only members of the families and a few friends attended. John Hayward was best man, and Jeannette's sister was the bride's only attendant. Immediately afterward Watson and his wife left for a long trip west, returning to Dayton at the end of May. As a wedding present Patterson gave them a summer house that he had built for them near his own country home. Five months later he fired Watson.

Patterson had a tendency to let other men dominate him, but only for a time. Just as a man began thinking himself indispensable, as had Palmer and Chalmers and a host of others, he would come to grief; for Patterson would suddenly, unpredictably, rebel against the very influence he had courted and put a swift and ultimate end to it. For years, in his deceptively meek manner, he might let a man have his way, stuttering, "Well, well, well, you ought to know best," then one day announce that there were only two things wrong with the fellow.

"Everything you do is wrong. Everything you say is wrong."

The end, although swift, was memorable and sometimes

cruel. Watson often told of the NCR executive who returned from a trip in the field to find his desk and chair on
the lawn in front of the factory. They had been soaked
with kerosene; and as he got out of his cab, they went up
in flames. Without a word the man got back in the cab and
drove away.

Inevitably it was fatal to attract Patterson's attention.
He fired some men because he was tired of them, others
because they annoyed him, a few probably just for recreation; but he always insisted that he had sound business
reasons for his ways. What looked like a casual squander-
ing of talent he defended as a method of preventing the
company from becoming dependent on any single person
— except, of course, himself.

John H. Patterson was a man who made men, said anyone who knew anything about him; but eventually, as he
grew older, it seemed that he was more interested in making men than cash registers. He ran a school for executives
in Dayton, promoting men from within the company,
training them and quickly advancing them; then, at the
height of their ability, he generously and arbitrarily sent
them off to work out his ideas in another industry.

The list of men he fired was, as someone once said,
"resplendent as a roll call in the House of Lords." Besides
the men he sent to the business machines industry, to the
automotive industry he gave Hugh Chalmers and E. S.
Jordan, president of the Jordan Motor Car Company;
Harry Ford and Lee Counselman, presidents of the Saxon
Motor Company; and Alvan Macaulay, president of the
Packard Motor Company. To DELCO, and hence to Gen-

eral Motors, he contributed R. H. Grant and C. F. Kettering.

With a thunderous faith in himself, Patterson watched the success of these other men without a qualm, but his whims had a price. The old man made men, it was true; but he would not keep them, and even though he must be credited with inspiriting American business with some of the most creative leadership of his time, the National Cash Register Company before his death began to lose ground and fall into a decline. Patterson eventually did admit one regret about his heads-off policy: that he had fired Thomas J. Watson.

Their relationship had grown difficult as Watson became more and more successful. Temperamentally the two were much alike — self-confident, with strong opinions, men who liked things done their own way. At first, however, Watson had been a master of tact, always sensing the right moment to give Patterson his head; but in time, perhaps misled by Patterson's deference to him in matters of sales policy, perhaps emboldened by the crisis of the trial, he had grown careless. Men who knew Patterson kept their disagreements with him private, to be aired during a horseback ride at Far Hills or a midnight chat before his fire. But Watson began disagreeing openly with the boss, arguing with him in front of other company officials and directors.

"I suppose you are right, Mr. Watson," was all that Patterson would say in his dangerously calm manner, but their relationship cooled, and tensions rose.

Patterson began to feel that he was being crowded toward the wings. He grew increasingly jealous of Watson's popularity with the sales force and saw sinister design in his promotion of his friends. Patterson fancied himself an expert on matters of salesmanship, as he undoubtedly was, and liked to act as sales manager whenever the position was vacant; but now he grew contemptuous of the office, telling his friends that selling cash registers took no special ability and that he was determined that a sales manager would never head up the National Cash Register Company.

Few needed these portents to see trouble ahead. Watson had been in office over five years, something of a company record, probably made possible by the fact that Patterson had been abroad almost half of that time.

Looking back afterward, some felt that the showdown began during the flood. In spite of Watson's shining achievement in mobilizing relief efforts and courting the press, Patterson used the occasion to air his mounting displeasure with his sales manager. Much to their surprise, Watson's assistants won all the praise, and the company rumor was that Watson had sent spoiled food to Dayton and had then ridden into town with the air of a man expecting acclaim.

Watson's troubles multiplied when he returned from his honeymoon. His right-hand man, Joe Rogers, had a nervous breakdown on the eve of the Hundred Point Club Convention in July; and he had to carry on alone. The convention was held in fine style with everyone in an ebullient mood, despite the outcome of the antitrust trial, which was never mentioned. Watson might have felt satisfied if an unsettling incident had not occurred. At the climax of his address, when the hall rang with applause, Patterson jumped to his feet to interrupt with irrelevant but portentous praise of a previous speaker, R. H. Grant, one of Watson's assistants. Patterson went on and on, ending Watson's remarks with obvious relish and underscoring his meaning by making one conspicuously short and spare reference to him.

A difference over sales policy was the occasion of the final break. Patterson decided to change a policy, and Watson opposed him, saying his idea would cut sales in half.

The company was his, Patterson raged, what right had Watson to care about what happened to it?

He had his business reputation at stake, Watson snapped back.

The battle was carried on in full view of the company, and at one time Patterson was so rude to Watson before the board of directors that Watson threatened to resign. When a reconciliation was offered, Watson went back to his desk, but nothing was the same afterward. There were few phone calls and little correspondence and no conferences with the president. Finally, within two or three weeks, Patterson asked him to leave, and at the end of November it was announced to the public that he and Joe Rogers had resigned. R. H. Grant became the new sales manager.

Watson was stunned. He had told people that he expected to get fired someday like the rest, but it was clear that he had not believed he would be. Now he was silent, for what could he say? The NCR was his life. It was his youth in Buffalo, it was riding into Rochester with Dexter and his rig. It was Jack Range and Meadville and the secondhand companies in Chicago. It was the exhilaration of making sales records, and salesmen talking far into the night, the smell of cigars, his old Pierce-Arrow, flags and tents at Far Hills, pep talks in St. Louis, and train rides and New York hotels. It was old Patterson with his easels and his bottled water and his pyramids and his genius. It was the trial and the flood. It was everything he was and for years everything he cared about. He was dispossessed.

Watson's friends were surprised at the way he met the situation. Walking away from his office for the last time, he stopped and looked back. With a gesture toward the buildings, the new School of Industrial Education, the auditorium, the additions to the factory, he said to the friends who were with him, "I've helped build all but one of those buildings. Now," he added, "I am going out to build a business bigger than John H. Patterson has."

He thought of Patterson's beginnings with the NCR. He had been over forty, with an indifferent career as a coal dealer behind him, when he started out in the cash register business with only $5000 capital. Now Watson, three months short of forty, faced his own challenge.

THE CTR

TWO TIMES in his life Watson showed greatness of spirit — once when he was an old man and when he left the National Cash Register Company. The second time he merely acquiesced in his fate, turning the inevitable into an act of will; but the first time was a bold, audacious act of spirit that contravened the circumstances of his life, defying and surmounting them. At forty he seemed a failure: disgraced, under jail sentence, with no job, no home, little money. And what success he had achieved in the past was modest, for what was the National Cash Register Company compared to giants like U.S. Steel, General Electric, and Standard Oil? And who was a sales manager, however brilliant his record, compared to men like Rockefeller and Morgan and Ford?

But Watson, standing astride personal misfortune, looked about himself and did not see defeat. He had his wife, steadfast, always believing in him, and now a son, born in January, 1914. And he had something more, a rare asset — courage. If it seemed to others that his career had been cut short, he saw only that it had been cut in two and that now, having been severed from the past, he had before him the future, and the future could mean only one thing — success.

There was something mystifying in this belief Watson had and would always have in himself. But baffling though it might be, it was the solid center of the man, self-generated, independent of circumstances, hard as bedrock. For more than six months he was out of a job, but never once during those dark days did he lose sight of his goal: in time he would be one of the great businessmen of his time.

He had many offers — from Frigidaire, Montgomery Ward, Remington Arms, a boat company in Connecticut, a Boston concern that made water coolers, even (or so it was said) a chance to manage the Dodge Motor Car Company. Some of these enterprises were substantial and the salaries big, but all they offered Watson was the middle way. Now that he had come to the real beginning of his career, he would settle for nothing less than command. And he wanted to make money. He would, he determined, work only for a commission, sharing in whatever profits his company made.

Other than a vision of greatness, Watson had no concept of what he wanted to do. When friends offered to finance him in any venture he decided to undertake, he had to admit that he had nothing in mind. Sometime late in the winter of 1913, someone suggested that he call on an Eastern financier who had organized a new business and was casting about for someone to run it. Watson went off to

New York to look into the matter, and so it was that he met one of the most colorful men in America, Charles R. Flint, financier, sportsman, pamphleteer, confidant of the mighty, *bon vivant*, and master of international intrigue.

Descended from a family of prosperous New England shipbuilders, he had begun his career with a shipping company dealing in the southern trade. Flint had the business instincts of his Yankee forebears, but the heart of an Elizabethan privateer, and it was easy for his interest to wander from bananas and guano to revolution. Before Watson was born, he was selling arms to South American republics; and at about the time Watson started school, he got involved in his first war, a small one between Peru and Chile. Characteristically he acted for both sides at one time or another; and thereafter he had a part in minor and major wars everywhere in the world as secret agent or munitions dealer, his specialty being trade in battleships. (He once equipped a belligerent with a complete navy in six weeks.)

If he won international fame for his mastery of naval supply, he made his name at home in a peaceable manner — by creating economic empires. While Watson was selling sewing machines in upper New York, Flint was bringing about his first industrial consolidation, the United States Rubber Corporation, and in the following decade he managed a brilliant succession of others, winning for himself the title of Father of Trusts.

He was by no means a simple man, this Flint; and Watson, arriving for their first meeting, was somewhat baffled. Twenty-five years his senior, Flint was a small man, urbane and articulate, afire with energy. But impatiently as he might snatch at the challenges of business and finance, he enjoyed a slow, oblique manner of sizing a man up, and there was no talk of business at breakfast that morning or afterward as the two men strolled two miles up Fifth Avenue to Flint's office. Nor was there any during their next few meetings, during which Flint let Watson come under the scrutiny of various colleagues. Nonetheless, Watson understood his intent, and tension mounted as Flint casually discussed cars or boats, hunting or horses.

When the conversation turned to business in his presence, it often became philosophical, for probably no one in America had thought as long or as profoundly as he about the changes the economy was then undergoing. Whereas John H. Patterson could effectively practice monopoly, Flint could justify it, or so he contended, arguing that monopolies benefited society, guaranteeing America's place as a world power through efficient mass production and distribution.

Flint expressed the spirit of his time when he said that the survival of the fittest "in the animal kingdom, in business and in the professions . . . was an inexorable law of life." And when he declared that "a combination of labor is a trades union, a combination of intelligence is a university, a combination of money is a bank — a combination of labor, intelligence and money is an industrial combination," President McKinley himself had applauded and ordered half a million copies of the speech for national distribution.

But McKinley belonged to the last century, and so, Watson knew, did some of Flint's ideas. The younger man may not have thought as long as Flint about the direction of the national economy, but he had given the problem of monopoly some concentrated attention in the past few months, and Flint was to find his ideas useful. Watson's experience had shown him some of the benefits of big business; the trial had illustrated some of its drawbacks. To Flint's positive-good theory of industrial combinations, Watson added his own ideas on the positive good of competition, and for all the power of the older man's arguments, he never lost faith in the opposing principle.

In his own good time Flint brought an end to generalities and broached the main matter on his mind — one of his consolidations, unlike any of the others in being a combination of what he called "allied interests," that is, manufacturers of similar but not identical products. The history of the enterprise went back to the turn of the century when he had consolidated the two infant industries of computing scales and time recorders. Even though thirteen companies were originally involved, the results were insignificant, but size was no gauge of Flint's interest; and seeing a link between the measurement of time and weight he negotiated a consolidation of these two combinations in 1911, drawing in, by the way, a third company almost as an afterthought, its inclusion more a tribute to Flint's passion for organization than logic, for it was not strictly related to the other two. It was the Tabulating Machine Company, a haphazard organization that produced a counting machine originally designed for dealing with census statistics. The new company, called the Computing-Tabulating-Recording Company, or the CTR, was not making money, and Flint had concluded that it needed new management. Watson, he decided, was his man.

There was some objection to him. When Flint put his proposition before his fellow directors, one bellowed, "What are you trying to do? Ruin this business? Who is going to run this business while he serves his term in jail?"

And when Watson was invited to a directors' meeting, someone began beligerently, "Why did you leave the NCR Company?"

"Because Mr. Patterson asked for my resignation," Watson replied.

Was it true that employees were required to ride horseback? was the next question. Watson talked freely about horses and cash registers and went on to express his admiration for Mr. Patterson despite his idiosyncracies and their differences of opinion. The directors were won by his manner, and a committee of three was appointed to negotiate terms.

Watson was frank with them. "I won't auction my services to anyone and believe that you gentlemen should make the proposition to me," he said. "I only want a 'gentleman's' salary and a part of the profits when I am able to make the company a success."

"In other words you want 'part of the ice you cut,'" Flint said slyly.

Watson agreed. The only reason that a small, obscure company like the CTR appealed to him at all was that it could provide him a chance to become an entrepreneur without capital, and so the only basis on which he considered the proposal was one that let him take over risks and rewards along with the management. Some thought him a fool, considering the company's poor earning record, but Flint was in complete sympathy with Watson's attitude, knowing that men of the first order of ability were not tempted by a fixed salary, but by the incentive of making a record and profiting by it.

Watson's salary was set at $25,000, and, in addition to an option on 1220 shares of stock, he was promised a profit-sharing arrangement, to be worked out in the future.

His new career did not begin auspiciously. A small-minded bookkeeper docked him three days' pay because he did not appear at his office at 25 Broad Street on May 1, 1914, the day he technically began working for the company. The fact that Watson was in Canada on company business made no difference. A few days earlier Watson had received notice that the board of directors was not going to elect him president of the company until the anti-trust case reached a conclusion in which, as the chairman of the board told him, "you will be relieved from any possible public discredit which might attach to it." In July the Supreme Court of Michigan found the NCR guilty of unlawful restraint of trade and fined the company $10,000, a grim portent of the possible outcome of the Federal case, then in the hands of the court of appeals.

Besides the natural antagonism that was to be expected by any newcomer in his position, Watson had to cope with the suspicion that the NCR trial engendered throughout the company. He met the situation head-on the first time he held a company meeting. His first speech was received coldly, with no applause, and the sense of the crowd was expressed by the man who said, "Perhaps there might be in the minds of some a feeling that the past holds more than the future."

Watson waited for someone else to bring up the question of competition. Then he rose to his feet and interrupted the proceedings.

". . . the only way that we want you men to handle the competition proposition is the only way we can afford to allow you men to handle it, that is, strictly on the merits of our goods. . . . You people when you come down to competition — must not do anything that's in restraint of trade, anything that will restrain the other fellow from selling his goods, anything that could be construed by anybody as unfair competition," he said, stammering in his earnestness. "You know, gentlemen, it is bad policy to do anything unfair with anybody, anywhere at any time, isn't it, in business or outside of business? No man ever won except in the one honest, fair and square way in which you men are working."

The audience burst into applause, interrupting Watson again and again as he assured them that he would uphold fairness no matter what the competition did.

". . . [A] splendid talk along the lines of clean, high-grade, fair and square dealing," declared the first salesman to speak out afterward. "It almost sounded sublime, but I am perfectly certain and fully convinced that it is sincere. . . . It is the biggest and best thing that I have heard so far in the entire convention. . . ." The spirit of the meeting quickened; and Watson, for the first time, began to take command.

Thereafter, he had little to say about competition except to remark that it was "the best supervisor a salesman can have" and caution his men to think about their own product, not the other fellow's. But he talked a great deal about cooperation. "Men exist for the sake of one another," he often said, quoting Marcus Aurelius. "Teach them then, or bear with them."

Before long the salesmen were singing:

> Mr. Watson is the man we're working for
> He's the leader of the CTR
> He's the fairest, squarest man we know.
> Sincere and true.
> He has shown us how to play the game
> And how to make the "dough."

Within three months of joining the company, Watson effectively demonstrated the sincerity of his stand by concluding an agreement between the Tabulating Machine Company and its competitor the Powers Accounting Company. Herman Hollerith, inventor of the tabulating machine, had been interested only in the electrical application of his idea; and when he failed to patent the mechanical version, his onetime foreman James Powers took up that line of development himself and before long had machines superior to Hollerith's. But the men backing Powers found that his system infringed several of Hollerith's patents.

"Mr. Watson, you are in a position to put us in business or put us out of business," Watson remembered one of them saying to him; and he always pointed out with pride that a license agreement was promptly concluded.

Later, when a fire destroyed Powers' card supply, Watson helped the company obtain card stock during the emergency.

These expressions and demonstrations of Watson's attitude about competition could do nothing to affect the outcome of the trial, upon which he and the directors of the CTR were keeping an anxious eye. In the fall of 1914 arguments began before the court of appeals with the government charging commercial piracy and the black flag in business. Both Watson and his friend Joe Rogers filed individual briefs, like the company basing their defense principally on the claim that the lower court had erred in ruling out evidence showing that the alleged illegal competition was undertaken against companies infringing NCR patents. In addition, Watson took the position that, as his brief put it, "Excessive zeal is a besetting sin of active and enterprising subordinates, but the excesses of a few over-zealous subordinates do not justify the inference that all members of the organization originally intended or subsequently approved and adopted such excesses."

Just before noon on March 13, 1915, Watson got a telegram from his father-in-law in Dayton, telling him that a verdict was expected momentarily. Watson went home to receive the news in private. An hour later word came: "District Court verdict set aside. New trial granted. Congratulations."

Although the matter was not concluded, the decision clearly indicated that the government would never be able to make the criminal indictment hold up before the courts.

Jubilation was Watson's reaction. "Shake, old man," he wired fellow defendants. "Come to New York, and I will buy you something nice."

"This decision has lifted a great load off my shoulders," he told a close friend. "Our Directors received the news of the Court's decision on Saturday afternoon, the 13th inst., and, on Monday morning, the 15th inst., they held a meeting, and elected me President and General Manager of the company."

Watson and his wife celebrated by going off to North Carolina for a vacation, free of the shadow of the courts for the first time since they met, or so it seemed. But as time went on, Watson was to find that he would never escape the trial, that it would work one way or another to shape his life thereafter. The issues that had been raised were basic to his time: the responsibility of a member of a group for the acts of the others; the conflict between rights conferred by the patent laws and limitations imposed by antitrust legislation; the slowly evolving questions about monopoly (Are large industrial combinations inevitable because of their effectiveness in meeting modern economic conditions, as Flint claimed? Or are they dangerous and avoidable?). Even when the NCR case was closed by a consent decree, these problems were not settled, at least not for Watson, nor would they be by the time of his death.

He refused to be party to the consent decree on the grounds that signing constituted an admission of guilt, and he always maintained that the fact the government did not undertake proceedings against him amounted to an exoneration. If he ever wondered what would have happened had he still been with the NCR, he did not say. But it was clear that his interpretation of the outcome of the trial did not satisfy him, and he was to spend the rest of his life building a career that would, by its moral fiber, answer the haunting indictment of the Federal court.

Knowing the shifting grounds of moral judgment upon which a business had to build, Watson could hope for only one certainty — command, the right to set the policies for which he was to be held responsible at that time or later. In the CTR the title of president did not assure him of that power, for the chief executive of the company was the chairman of the board, George W. Fairchild, one of the original financiers of the time recording business. By the time of the merger of the CTR he had made a comfortable fortune in various business ventures and a name for himself in Congress, and he was a natural choice for command. A big, imposing man with a generous mustache and heavy hair parted uncompromisingly in the middle, he resembled a nearsighted, mild Teddy Roosevelt. Like Roosevelt he had strong opinions and in addition, with his large holdings in the company, an entrenched position that made him one of the major factors in Watson's life for the next ten years.

Watson's experience had schooled him in dealing with men like Fairchild. In fact, his capacity for tact, refined by the setbacks he had recently experienced, was never higher than during those first few difficult years with the CTR, nor would he ever again be called upon to display it with greater skill and patience.

Noting that Fairchild was sensitive about his position in the company, Watson always made a special point of consulting him, saying, "I want you to feel that I will do everything in my power to act in accordance with your ideas . . . and I will keep you fully posted in regard to everything." Or again, "I greatly appreciate your judgment, advice and help in all matters." Gradually Fairchild was won over to Watson as his ability became plain, but the two had some sharp differences over policy, once over a matter of first importance.

"If you want me to come in here and operate this business for the benefit of the business, I'll do it, but I will not have anything to do with the operation of it from a stock standpoint," Watson had originally told the board, and they had agreed. But some looked upon the CTR, which was, after all, a holding company, as little more than a financial arrangement, an opportunity for quick profit through stock manipulation. They had no sympathy for Watson's plans, which meant the sacrifice of immediate profits for the long-range benefit of the business. Fairchild went along with them to the extent of wanting the company to resume dividends, which had lapsed at the beginning of 1914. Watson, on the other hand, wanted to put all profits back into the business for the time being. On his side was Flint, and he prevailed.

Flint helped Watson through another crisis at about the same time. Watson found that powerful interests had